the mutt manuscripts

Megan McFarlane

Megan McFarlane

Megan McFarlane

OTHER TITLES BY MEGAN MCFARLANE

if it falls on the floor, it's mine!

Megan McFarlane

DEDICATION

To my wonderful husband, Malcolm – with tail wagging love!

An advertisement promising love brought me you,
An ad for a puppy promising adventure brought us Tiamo.
I am so grateful all the promises have come true!

Megan McFarlane

CONTENTS

Megan McFarlane

ACKNOWLEDGMENTS
&
TAIL WAGS

Tail wags are a special gift from our canines. I can look over at one of the girls as they are laying down, make eye contact, and their tails will give me a thump-thump against the bricks of our floor. Their message of love, of comfort, of feeling is all conveyed in that thump-thump of their tail. It's a quick, "luv 'ya!" sent via a white-tipped tail whack.

There are several extraordinary people I would like to send out special tail wags to. A few are mentioned throughout the book, some are in the background behind the scenes and some are blatantly cited.

To all our many guests and visitors, neighbors and friends, family and like family, co-workers and acquaintances, that have graciously given your friendship throughout the years. You know exactly who you are. You have put up with our rambunctious dogs since they were roly-poly little puppies, lived through their unmanageable teenage years, and have embraced their quieter adult years. You have pulled stray dog hairs out of your wine glass and have left our house covered in black fur. You have loved our dogs, sent them Christmas bones and Big Dog water bowls for presents. You have endured our doggy picture brag book, listened to our dog stories, and dutifully inquired of our girls. You recognized Tiamo, Dolce and Amore are our canine children and rightfully treated them as so.

In no particular order: Jim and Darlene, Nelson, Dan from D.C., Dick and Terry, Jonnalyn, Aunt Dee, Josh and Liz, Margaret, Greg and Laura, Mayra, Ellen, Tara, Mink, Ken and Beth, Doug and Walter, Aggie, Allyson, Blair, Missy. I love you all!

IT STARTED WITH TIAMO

Born on thanksgiving, Tiamo was a birthday present to my husband when he turned fifty. Within minutes of her arrival to her new home with us, she had Malcolm and myself wrapped around all of her soon-to-be very huge paws. All four of them! We were smittened.

Tiamo completed our family. Husband, wife, dog. We were set.

However, life as we knew it just changed. Big time. Like parents of a newborn, sleep was a thing of the past, eating dinner together was no longer an option and we said goodbye to afternoon naps. Tiamo demanded attention. A lot of attention. Constant attention. She did NOT like being ignored. At all!

Tiamo was an early bird. She demanded being fed early in the morning at the crack of dawn. Five a.m. early. She commandeered the day from the minute she woke to when she put her head on the pillow to sleep. We were on her schedule.

She was our everywhere dog. Wherever we went, she went and we brought her everywhere. Malcolm, Tiamo and I made three. Not just for trips into town. We brought Tiamo with us on vacation, to the office on weekends, and even shopping. We planned travel and adventures around Tiamo. We stayed at hotels that accepted pets, and let me tell ya', you get the worse room ever. We investigated parks and beaches that allowed dogs, with and without leashes. We found restaurants and cafes that had outdoor eating. We made friends because of Tiamo. People adored her, we just plain loved her.

Everyday was a new adventure for Tiamo. There were cookbooks to chew, magazines to rip up and wooden spoons to carry from room to room. Friends would fight over who held Tiamo's leash on walks. Neighborhood kids would randomly drop by to pet her and give her more love. Tiamo loved every minute of her life. She was the star and damn if she didn't know it.

Even Malcolm and I would argue over who loved her more. She was the darling of our neighborhood, the community and our hearts. Everyone loved Tiamo and Tiamo loved us all.

Tiamo knew not to beg for table scraps, but she was quick to lick up any tasty tidbit that fell to the floor. With dogs, you have less than a nano-second to claim ownership of dropped food scraps. Otherwise, the fallen treasure is all theirs, gulped down faster then a blink of an eye with their snout sniffing for more. People with dogs often use the "dog" rule. If it falls on the floor, no worries, the dog will lick it up quick, cleaning the floor in the process.

We learned Tiamo had a keen ability to counter-surf, quickly and quietly. Cartons of cream would go missing, only to be found empty in another room. Cookies cooling on racks on the kitchen counter would be one fewer of a dozen. Licked-clean butter plates would be discovered under couch pillows. Tiamo had the gold medal on counter-surfing. She was a pro!

Then she was busted – caught in the act with one paw reaching for the goods! At two in the morning, we were awakened by a big crash; Tiamo had jumped up on the kitchen table to lick up leftover dinner crumbs.

Anyone who has ever owned a dog has had a similar experience; turning your back for just a few minutes, resulting in missing ingredients while cooking and an innocent look from the beloved pooch that says, "Who me?" That was our Tiamo.

Tiamo was a magnet for children and adults both. Our nephew, Sam, would "borrow" her, taking her for walks around the local college campus with high hopes of picking up cute coeds. Allow her in the front seat of the car and we would receive no less than five friendly honks at a stoplight and at a minimum, four thumbs up when other drivers would take notice of her.

Tiamo had personality, good looks, charm and charisma. In spades. She used it to her advantage. Don't get me wrong, Tiamo was as sweet and gentle as can be, but that girl worked it! A gentle nose nudge would garner a multitude of loving.

Tiamo was our dog clock. She let us know when it was time to go on our walks, to eat and to go to sleep. Her day started at five in the morning and didn't stop until evening. At 5:10 p.m. on the dot, Tiamo would stand by the front door wanting out. She would sit beside the front portal gate watching, waiting for me to arrive home from work. At 8:30 p.m., she came down to the den, backing up as she barked, telling me it was time for me to come to bed. She knew when the mailman arrived, when the newspaper was tossed and she always knew when something good might be cooking.

With an average lifespan of seven to ten years, Berners aren't known for their longevity. Malcolm and I knew when it came Tiamo's time to leave us we would be heartbroken. After many discussions, we decided to bring another Bernese Mountain Dog into our household. A puppy a few years younger that could also be a companion for Tiamo.

The only problem was Tiamo didn't like the idea of sharing us. We were hers and she was ours. No little whippersnapper was going to come between us. In the course of her first twelve months, Tiamo had become very territorial. Play dates with neighborhood canines turned into boxing matches between the two canines with Malcolm and I playing referee. Doggy sitting for friends was no longer doable. Tiamo had a fit when another dog held our attention. We were in a dilemma.

Tiamo loved other dogs when meeting up on a hike and while visiting friends, but not on her home turf. She liked having Malcolm and I to herself. The decision was made to breed her, with plans to keep one of her litter puppies. We knew it would be the only way she would accept another dog in our home and in her life. So we started the long process of researching, studying, waiting and testing.

Berners have a long history of hip dysplasia. Careful breeding and testing is critical when procreating the breed. At two years, a Bernese Mountain Dog should be tested for a hip/shoulder/elbow grade through the Orthopedic Foundation for Animals (OFA). OFA is a non-profit organization that collates and disseminates information concerning orthopedic and genetic disease of animals.

While the OFA continues to focus on hip dysplasia, today's OFA Mission, "To improve the health and well being of companion animals through a reduction in the incidence of genetic disease," reflects the organization's expansion into other inherited diseases. When Tiamo turned two, we sent off specially taken x-rays to be reviewed and graded. She passed. It was now time to find her a boyfriend and daddy for her future pups.

From the time Tiamo was a little puppy, she was a flirt. She loved men, and she loved older Bernese males. She could charm herself into any situation of her making. If we happened to run into a male Berner while out and about, Tiamo immediately would puff out her chest, put an extra swish in her tail and bat her big brown eyes. Put a little yap dog in front of her and her eyes would glaze over with boredom. But a big masculine Bernese Mountain Dog was a whole other story.

Finding the perfect father for Tiamo's future litter wasn't the problem, finding a perfect intact male Berner that lived near by was.

As luck would have it, we did locate a handsome male Bernese Mountain Dog. With champion bloodlines, Gus, a handsome strapping young lad, stepped up to the plate and became the father of Tiamo's litter. We had met Gus's human folks months earlier while out with Tiamo. When we learned Gus had all the right equipment, we knew we had found our boy! With the human folk's permission, we just waited for Tiamo to mature and grow up.

When we bred Tiamo, the whole neighborhood was part of the pregnancy. Kids from the neighborhood would stop by, checking to see if the puppies had arrived. Next-door neighbors offered assistance when the day came and wanted to be called the minute her water broke, when she was ready for delivery. It was a community project. Project Tiamo. Everyone was involved.

At four weeks, she had a sonogram, which revealed four puppies. I'll never forget how excited Tiamo was. I had taken her to the vet and after I received the news to expect four little puppies, I stopped at the pet store on the way home to purchase four teeny-weeny puppy collars. A different color for each collar. One for each of our future puppies. Placed in a paper bag, I handed the sack to Tiamo for her to carry into the house.

She grabbed the bag in her gentle jaws and promptly trotted up to Malcolm, dropping the bag at his feet. Not sure what was going on, Malcolm ignored the bag. Determined, our proud mama picked up the bag again only to drop it once more at Malcolm's feet, barking just once to get his attention. That did it.

Malcolm picked up the paper sack and peered inside. His dumbfounded look was priceless.

"Four? We're going to have four puppies?" he asked.

The idea that we were soon to have a house full of puppies hit home. Shock set in. Four? That quickly, I swear I saw his blonde head of hair go a shade or two lighter. The stork was going to deliver sixteen paws in another four weeks. We were excited, expectant parents, eagerly waiting for our babies.

After confirming her pregnancy, the next weeks were all about taking care of our new mom-to-be. We read every book, every article, conducted web searches on canine pregnancies and took every precaution. Tiamo was fed a nutrient rich diet, we continued her daily walks, although they were less strenuous and shorter distances. Every night during her pregnancy, I gave Tiamo gentle belly rubs to soothe her muscles, a ritual that continued on a daily basis to her dying day. The house was made puppy proofed. We were ready.

As Tiamo's due date came closer, as she grew bigger and bigger, it became harder and harder for her to maneuver up on the couch or on the bed. I would crawl down on the hard brick floor to rub her swollen tummy, massaging her muscles, easing her discomfort. Tiamo was one of the most relaxed moms-to-be I had ever seen. Her pregnancy and delivery was textbook easy and stress-free. I, of course, credit it all to the belly rubs I performed.

Like the sweetheart she was, Tiamo waited until mid-morning on a Labor Day weekend Saturday for her water to break. No 3:00 a.m. rush to the vet hospital, no siree bob! No middle-of-the-week-have-to-be-at-work-in-three-hours delivery. No outside in the freezing temperatures, no hiding in the darkest corner of her pen. Just your average delivery. Piece of cake.

She waited until a reasonable hour, an hour that she knew we would be up, an hour that had already provided us two cups of strong coffee and a chance to read the morning paper. Tiamo waited until 10 o'clock in the morning before she climbed into her whelping pen and gave the world her beautiful puppies. Like clock work, her little puppies came one after another.

However, the sonogram was wrong. She didn't have four

puppies, she had eight! Eight puppies. We went from sixteen little paws to thirty-two. Seven females and one male. Good lord, eight! We were prepared for four puppies, now we had double the trouble.

We had found families for first four puppies, ourselves and three others. Now we needed to find homes for the additional four pups. Our work was cut out for us.

We placed an advertisement in the local papers and waited for a response. Calls came in. Questions asked. Can we come a see the little puppies? When will they be ready to leave their mother? How much care will they require? We carefully interviewed the prospective canine caregivers. These were Tiamo's little ones, we weren't going to let them go to just any home. We needed to reassure ourselves the puppies would be going to a safe and secure environment. An attentive family that would love and cherish them.

Tiamo's litter consisted of eight of the most adorable puppies. All healthy, all roly-poly. We religiously weighed each puppy daily, changed out their whelping pen with clean bedding, and made sure Mama had a break from her kids. We were enraptured with the little ones.

Malcolm and I watched over them as they gained strength, moving around the enclosed whelping pen. We tracked the litter as each puppy began to open their eyes, as each one discovered their voice. Malcolm and I made sure each puppy had their fair share of nursing and carefully monitored their feeding as the litter switched over to puppy chow.

At four weeks old, the little pups were moved out of the house and into the garage where we built a huge enclosure for them. All cars were now parked in the driveway. It was their nighttime pen. Safe and out of the elements, the garage pen was designed for their comfort and ours.

For the first time since they were born, we had a quiet night of sleep. No little mewing or barks. No tiny yips or puppy growls. No scratching noises from little paws taking a try at escape from the whelping pen. It was peace and quiet. All nightlong. All blessed nightlong. Our puppy euphoria was starting to tire.

During the warm fall days of late September and October, we brought the puppies outside to our "outdoor pen." Mama would watch over the puppies as they ventured into new territory. Malcolm and I would sit inside the pen and quietly observe Tiamo's family. We chuckled and laughed over their antics. We watched the pups grow. We took picture after picture after picture and immediately added the photos to our desktop on our computers. We were proud parents.

Weeks five through eight brought new adventure into their lives. The pups tumbled and toppled over each other as they played in the outdoors. They discovered new scents as they explored their surroundings. They ate and ate and grew and grew. And there were eight of them!

There is nothing that will melt your heart faster than eight puppies running towards you as your enter the pen. Each trying to out run the others to reach us first. There is nothing more precious than holding two to four wriggling, squirming little puppies in your arms as they endeavor to lick your face and nibble on your ear. There is nothing better than seeing the joy and happiness shining from their bright eyes as they live life. Let's face it, there is nothing better than eight beautiful Bernese puppies.

By week ten, most of the litter had been sent home to their new families. There were just two puppies left. Ours and an extra. Our temporary canine family was emptying but fast. Tiamo was glad to get back to status quo. Personally, I think she was tired of sharing our attention and wanted life back the way it was B.P. Before Puppies.

Both Malcolm and I were suffering from Empty Nest Syndrome. We missed our little ones. For ten weeks, Tiamo and her litter of pups had been our life. Everything we did was geared around Tiamo and the puppies. We were now waving goodbye to our dear treasured kids. We had one last puppy to find a home for.

We tried. Hard. But our extra puppy kept coming back to us. Just when we thought we had a good family willing to watch over our "extra," her future home fell through. Three times we thought we had the perfect family for our "extra" little girl and three times our little puppy stayed right where she was. With us. We were stuck.

By week sixteen, our extra puppy was staying put. We were head over paws in love with our now two puppies and couldn't bare the thought of not having either one in our lives. We kept both, enlarging our family to one cat, two humans and three dogs. Three very large Bernese Mountain Dogs. Three, 100 pounds each, with canine drool and wagging tail dogs.

We ended up with two of Tiamo's puppies, Amore and Dolce, enriching our lives even more. Although raising two puppies along with mom has been quite the adventure, we wouldn't trade it for a single moment nor trade any paw.

We have been truly blessed with our dog family.

OUR FIRST

A MORE is our little "first"!

She was, and still is, our "first-at-everything" puppy. She was the first pup to arrive in our world, the first to crawl, the first to climb out of the whelping pen, the first to bark, the first to jump and the first to start mischief! Mutt mischief. That's a lot of firsts.

Tiamo's litter was only three weeks old when I needed to travel for work. I was going to be away for only five days, but a lot could happen in five days. Especially with a new litter of puppies.

Malcolm was confident he would be able to handle "mama and the kids" while I was absent. Dick, a neighbor from across the way had offered to help Malcolm should he need anything. Tiamo was proving to be a great mom, ensuring all the puppies were properly fed, bathed and tended to. For new puppy parents, our first three weeks had been relatively easy. The glow of parenthood was still in its first phase of wonderment.

The first day I was away, Malcolm reported all was well. Dick had stopped by to see the kids and Malcolm promptly put him to work in assisting the weigh-in of the pups. They were doing well. Gaining weight, their eyes had opened to a dark blue, and they were strengthening their chubby little legs as they waddled around in their whelping pen. Tiamo was attentive to their needs. Life was good.

It was the following days when reality hit. Amore had found her vocal cords and we found she had a healthy set of lungs. Fully exercising them at 2:30 a.m. in the morning, Malcolm was awakened by a high-pitched yap. It was Amore. The first puppy to bark. He jerked out of bed, turning lights on as he climbed out. There was Amore, her little head peaking over the rim of the whelping pen, paws grabbing purchase on the top edge. Wide-eyed and bushy tailed, Amore wanted attention.

The next night, Malcolm awoke to a piercing shrill penetrating his sleep. Frantic puppy cries had him worried Tiamo was crushing one of the puppies, suffocating a little one. Instead, there was Amore, on the wrong side of the pen, having climbed out of the whelping pen. Missing her siblings, she wanted back. Amore had another "first" under her belt. She was the first puppy to climb out of the whelping pen. It was the onset of chaos. Puppy chaos.

"We're not keeping that one!" Malcolm greeted me as I walked in the door upon my return from my trip, pointing to little Amore. No welcome home kiss, no "how was your trip."

"She barks! All night long! She crawled out of the whelping pen. She is going to cause us nothing but trouble!" he added as he pointed to the offensive little pup.

"We are NOT keeping her!" he ranted once more for good measure. I looked from him to Amore and back at Malcolm. From the supposedly mature adult to our tiny little puppy. From the grown-up sternly expressing his opinions, making his views known to me, to the most adorable little pup, sitting on its haunches, its head tilted to the side, tail a-wagging, with a roly poly tummy. As you can guess, the puppy won this battle. We kept Amore. Amore had just won her first battle. Another check mark in the "first" column.

Amore' is our hyperactive child. She loves to run, just for the joy of running. Full of high-energy, she has three speeds: 1) idling with the engine revving, eyes alert and her tail a-wagging, anxiously waiting for something to happen; 2) tail in the air, speeding through life. Why walk when you can run through the house, land on a rug and get a free ride into the living room? Weeeeeeee, look at meeeee! CRASH!; and, 3) crashing into a fast sleep, dead to the world while she recharges her batteries for more excitement when she wakes up.

Amore is the first to wake up, demanding to be fed, insistent for one of us to be awake along side her. She takes after Tiamo in that regard. Ignoring her does no good. If Amore wants you awake, up and att'em, you are up!

She loves the snow and making snow angels, biting at the snow as she rolls over. She loves to ride in the car, head hanging out the window, ears flapping. Loves to chase lizards and bunnies and the low-flying shadows of the many birds in our area. Loves to jump in a pool of water and shake to see where the water drops fall. Loves to eat apples picked from our fruit trees and loves to tease Malcolm. Simply put, Amore loves life! She brings us joy and smiles.

When Malcolm takes the girls for a quick trip to the grocery store, Amore explodes from the back end of the SUV, jumping into the driver's seat as he exits from the car. On full alert, she is ready for a fast get-away as she impatiently waits for his return. She'll sit there, never taking her eyes off the store's entrance, eager for Malcolm's reappearance.

Amore in the driver's seat, Dolce riding shotgun, makes Bonnie and Clyde look like novices. People walking by, see two look-alike Berners sitting respectively in their appointed front seat positions, sometimes with a paw strategically placed on the steering wheel. It's a chuckle and never fails to bring smiles to the passerbys.

With shiny, bright eyes, Amore greets each morning before sunrise, ready to run through the day at full speed.

We kept our little "first." A pistol for sure, a handful, absolutely, but such a joy in our lives and well worth the adventure.

THE DOLCH

The "Dolch." Dolce was our extra. We weren't planning on keeping two puppies, but somehow, Dolce kept returning to us. Her home was with us.

Dolce was one of the more diminutive pups in the litter. Not quite the runt, but definitely not on the larger side. Despite her size, from day one, she was determined to be next to me or on me. She might have been one of the smallest in the litter, but she also was the most determined puppy.

When we took the puppies to the vet for their first set of shots, somehow, she somehow ended up on my lap while driving to the clinic. From then on, by nook or by cranny, Dolce was on my lap. Being the smallest did not deter her. She could nose her way past her littermates and finagle her way on my lap without much of a struggle. She has been my 100-pound lap dog ever since.

When our litter of Berner puppies were barely two days old and just about a pound each, we bundled them up in a padded, warm carrier, and along with mamma, brought them in to the vet's to have their dew claws removed. If removed in the first week of life, dew claws are still soft like a fingernail and can be removed relatively easily with no stitches required.

I sat in the back seat to keep an eye on the pack while Malcolm drove into town to the clinic. Tiamo kept an careful eye on me, not trusting and unsure of the process, she was an anxious mamma, agitated we were moving her pups. Three hours later we were back home, the lil' tykes happily nursing, Tiamo calm now that she had her puppies under her care. It was Dolce's first car ride and the beginning of her love affair with my lap.

Eight weeks later we brought them back to the vet's for their first set of shots – DHPP, which includes Distemper, Parvo, Parainfluenza, and Heartworm prevention.

Malcolm had prepped our SUV, the back seats laid down and lined with a tarp for "puppy accidents," he loaded up eight roly-poly, tail-wagging, wiggling little puppies, each weighing from the low-to-high twenties', into the car. For the puppies, not counting the trip to the vet's to remove their dewclaws; it was their first official car ride, a new adventure in a new setting.

With Malcolm driving, I rode shotgun, half-turned in my seat to keep an eye on the dear little souls. Eight little noses immediately started sniffing and exploring the inside of the car. Tails straight up, their little noses wrinkling, as they would catch a new and unfamiliar scent. They searched out every corner in the car.

Dolce was the first explorer to find her way up into the front seat territory. She started with two white-capped paws on the hard leather console; her back paws still on the edge of the back seat. Wobbling between the padded edge of the folded down back seat and the middle armrest between the front seats, she tried to advance. She had a nano second before falling.

Stretched out and stuck fast, I caught her just as she was about to do a backwards somersault into the black hole called the floor. I reached out and placed her on my lap. Safe and secure, she nestled in between my legs, occasionally standing to peek out the window, only to plop back down on my lap with a contented sigh. Dolce was hooked. From that moment on, Dolce has had a fascination with the front seat and sitting on my lap.

Bigger and heavier by many pounds, by the third month, most of the puppies had left for their new homes, leaving Amore and Dolce, the two puppies we kept. It was time for another round of shots, their DHPP booster and their Bordetella, Lepto and Lyme vaccines, requiring another trip to the vet's.

Once again, Malcolm folded the back seats down, laid a tarp over the back-end and loaded up the girls. As they muscled their way around the car, excited to be on another car ride, I climbed into the front passenger seat.

I had barely clicked my seat belt before I felt a cold wet nose nudging my elbow. Wiggling under my arm, Dolce had barreled her way onto my lap. Thirty-five pounds of determined canine snuggled up on my lap, her paws hanging over my knees, her tail happily whacking Malcolm's right arm as he drove. Dolce had once again found her favorite spot – my lap.

As Dolce and Amore continued grow, so did their love of riding in the car to travel. Using the 65 rule, the equation is simple: 6 months old = 65 lbs. = 65 mph = a 65 minute round-trip in the car = Dolce sitting at a sixty-five degree angle on my lap.

As soon as they hear the car keys jingle, they are out the door and in the car, with Dolce readily claiming dibs on the front seat, riding shotgun. All under 6.5 seconds. I have to scoot Dolce over just to sit down. She'll wait for the click of the seat belt and be right back on my lap two seconds later. Her seat is my lap.

There is no such thing as "sneaking out" to go to the store. Words such as "CAR," "STORE" and "TOWN" have to be spelled out or written down. By the time Dolce was 65 pounds, she didn't even come close to fitting on my lap. At all. Though uncomfortable and cramped, she was and still is, bound and determined to park herself between the console and the passenger door with me sitting underneath. There are times when I purposely sit in the back seat, allowing Dolce the full acreage of the front seat.

Dolce was our extra puppy. She was the puppy that kept coming back to us. We would think we had her placed in a good home, interview the family to ensure she would be in a safe environment and carefully watch Dolce interact with her new family. Before we could deliver Dolce to her new home, the potential new owners would back out, unable to care for her for some reason or another.

Three times we thought we found a home for her and three times Dolce stayed right where she wanted to be. With us. On my lap.

By the time Dolce was 16 weeks old, Malcolm and I couldn't part with her. Just like how she inched her way onto my lap, Dolce had inched her way into our hearts. She was part of our family and her place was with us. We couldn't part with our extra. There was no way we would let her go. By January, we admitted we now had three Bernese Mountain Dogs. Tiamo, Amore and now Dolce.

We had no idea what we were getting ourselves into. Were we crazy? What were we thinking? Three dogs. Holy-guacamole! Three large beautiful Bernese Mountain Dogs that require a lot of attention and a lot of care. Were we out of our minds? Three 100-pound lap dogs all wanting on my lap at the same time, all fighting for squatter's rights. Yes, we were crazy! Trust me, we were crazy! YES. WE. WERE. CRAZY!

When Dolce was 6 months, she needed surgery on both shoulders. While recovering, Dolce would sit on the sidelines with Malcolm and myself and watch Tiamo and Amore play. Wanting some attention of her own, Dolce became our big ol' huge ol' cuddle bug. She would stretch out over my lap, rolling over to expose her underside, looking up at us with innocent beguiling eyes, in high hopes of a tummy rub. Without us even being aware of it, we would end up rubbing her belly, or scratching her ear.

She is a first class finagler. Dolce knows just the right move, just the right position, just the right nudge that will give her all the rubs, all the petting she wants. That girl loves her rubs and hugs!

Dolce loves to carry "things" around the house and out to the pen. Give her a bone and she'll carry it from room to room as she follows us throughout the house. She will spend hours gnawing on a bone until we have to take it away from her, tossing it before it becomes splintered.

Kongs are her favorite. Present her with a peanut butter filled Kong and she is happy for days while she licks at her treat.

However, she does not share. What's hers is hers. Afraid Tiamo or Amore will steal her valuable treasures; Dolce tucks her special stash of goods under her front legs, with her head lowered over the bundle. A low warning growl issued to keep the other two from trying to wrestle her prize away.

Not that the other two don't try. We've broken up quite a few dog spats over a bone or Kong. It's so obvious when Amore will filch a bone just to tease Dolce. Should Amore see a chance to steal away a toy or treat from Dolce's possession, she will, and immediately run out to the pen with it, away from Dolce.

Dolce has perfected the art of "Mow, Blow and Go." To our dismay, Dolce has become quite knowledgeable in the procedures of opening doors. That's the mow part. Any door she can pretty much mow down, but her specialties are garage doors, front doors, and closet doors. She'll mow over anything in her way.

No door is sacred, nor is any object found on the other side. That's the blow part. To Dolch, a closed door equals something good might be found. A special treasure to "Grab n' Nab." Close the closet door as you leave the room and it will be wide open upon your return. Does she think we don't know it is her taking things? That the wind just blows it away?

Dolce once dragged a heavy winter parka from one end of the house, out to the pen. Missing a shoe from your closet, check the pen. Not to chew, but just because she could. That's the go portion. Wave goodbye, it's gone.

We have had to install double-locks on the garage door and place a bolt high on the front entry. Chairs are strategically placed in front of the back glass slider when we leave the house to block Dolce from opening the door.

Houdini at her best, Dolce is way too smart. She can turn the dead bolt with her paws and push the door open. For her return, she just uses her muzzle to pull the door towards her and quickly enters back through before it swings back shut. I can't tell you how many times we've heard the door out to the garage bang open and slam shut at 2:30 a.m.

Of the three dogs, Dolce is the most passive. But not when it comes to her Kong or loading up into the car. She could be twenty yards behind the other two, but it's a sure bet she'll be in the car and positioned on my lap in the front seat before either Tiamo or Amore can even think about jumping up into the car. To this day, Dolce is always first in the car and first on my lap. I now get in the car and buckle up before I allow Malcolm to let the dogs in. It's a sight for other drivers when they pass us.

Full grown at 98 pounds, today, Dolce is one of the sweetest dogs. She comes up on the bed for a nighttime cuddle session before she settles down on her own doggy bed on the floor. She still wants the front seat of the car (passenger beware). Head scrunched down, rear end just barely sitting on the arm rest, paws dangling down to the floor board, drivers passing us look with open mouth awe as they look through into the front window and see the sight. A 100-pound lap dog as happy as can be. And, she still continues to sit on my lap no matter where we are.

Dolce has lived up to her name, she is our little sweetheart!

Megan McFarlane

WHO'S WHO....?

What started as a search for a companion dog for Tiamo, took us through a litter of eight and landed us with two new additions to our household. Three dogs.

We quickly became known as "those crazy dog people" that lived down the road. And, we have pretty much lived up to our reputation.

"Oh, you're the ones with the dogs," new neighbors will comment when we meet them for the first time. It gets a bit embarrassing. The knowing looks sent our way, the avoidance when we pass on the road. You know it is bad when someone picks up their little dog to hold in their arms as we walk past them, protecting their pooch as the girls excitedly run up to greet them.

People often ask us how we tell the "girls" apart. Sometimes even we get confused. Like with twins, sometimes only a parent knows. And sometimes it's a mystery. From behind, it can be anyone's guess who is who. Straight on, there are subtle clues as to which one is which.

When the girls were little, the mystery usually resulted in Dolce being accused of something Amore did or Tiamo getting away with a no-no. When they were puppies, we never knew which one had committed the crime. Today we know they are all in cahoots together.

There are times when we have to lift up one of their tails, checking the white painted tip at the end to determine if it's Dolce or Amore who is the culprit. Dolce has almost no white at the tip of her tail while Amore has a good three inches of solid snow.

If the two are side by side facing us, Dolce has a much thinner blaze down her forehead. Narrow and jagged, there is a hint of Harry Potter in her striped mark. Amore is a bit taller and has a more of a square profile.

It was easier to tell them apart when Amore and Dolce were puppies and Tiamo was the mature canine. When Dolce had shoulder surgery, the shaved area over her shoulders was a sure clue as to which one she was. For several months, the sheared shoulders were rather prominent and made life easier. As the two of them grew, gained weight and developed, it became a struggle to determine which one was Tiamo, Amore or Dolce.

Debbie, our puppy sitter once told us, "One of the girls didn't eat all of her dinner."

"Which one?" we asked.

"Um, I'm not sure, it might have been Amore, um, or maybe it was Dolce," she hesitated in her reply.

She'll then ask, "which one has the larger white blaze on her face?" Mystery solved, Amore.

Tiamo, the mother, had a deep-barreled chest and a more queenly stature. She had a prance in her walk, like a model strutting down the catwalk. Tiamo was a charmer. Well-behaved and gentle, she loved children, people and most other cats and dogs. Tiamo had a large ruff of fur around her neck, giving her a stately royal physique. She was regal. All I had to do was look into her eyes and I could tell it was Tiamo.

If Tiamo liked you, she would lean up against your legs, nuzzling your hand for a friendly caress. If she loved you, she would come up from behind and push her way through your legs, lifting her head once she found an opening for an ear scratch or a neck rub. She knew she was our "girl." The matriarch within the hierarchy of the dogs, she ruled the doghouse and us. She was our queen.

Amore has a lot more spice in her personality. Always on the go, always has to run. She is the one who gulps her food down the fastest and the one who has seen the inside of the vet's office the most. She is the tallest of the three dogs by two to three inches and the leanest by five pounds. She has a wild spark in her eyes that defies description. Bright, shiny, Amore's eyes glow with happiness. Out of the three of them, Amore is the only one that grins. A goofy grin that looks more like a grimace, one side of her muzzle pulling up, almost a snarl. But with those shinny eyes and a wildly wagging tail, we see her smile. Pure joy.

Amore has total disregard for anything in her way. For her, the fastest way is through it, or, once in a while, over it. She will sit on anything, the tiniest ledge, the smallest gap, the most uneven surface, if that is where she wants to be. Unfortunately, it's usually on our cat, Gordita. Or on my feet.

Amore knows no boundaries. That's not saying she isn't well mannered or trained (ok, maybe not the best well-mannered or trained canine), it's just that Amore believes in straight-line travel.

On the other hand, Dolce is our sweetheart. With a thin white stripe on her forehead and maybe, at best, three strands of white hairs on her tail, Dolce likes to hang with the old folks. She stays close to us on hikes, always checking our GPS status, never straying too far ahead on the trail. She wants to always know where we are.

Her eyes are soft, sweet even. When I give her belly rubs, she'll close her eyes in ecstasy. You just know she is in heaven. Content. In mannerisms, she is the more like Tiamo. And like Tiamo, Dolce loves her tummy rubbed.

Dolce is our thinker. She wants to ensure it is worth her while before she makes a move. You can almost see the scales tipping in her head as she weighs the pros and cons of her next move.

If Dolce hears the refrigerator door open, she'll cock her head, lift an ear, waiting for the crinkle of a cheese wrapper before deciding to make a shift in her position. When she hears the jug of milk being lifted, she'll plop back down, false alarm.

She'll wait, deciphering the noises, the clatter, and the sounds. She'll sit up, looking intently at the scene, scanning the situation, evaluating her options. Should she or shouldn't she move off the sofa. Dolce is not lazy by any means, she just makes sure any shift or movement is the best option and worth the effort.

But she is always first out the door and in the car.

… So, if you don't know which dog is with you, just love the one you're with.

IT MEANS "SWEETHEART"

February. The month of love. The month of romance. The month everyone, of every age, wants to feel special and loved and showered with purple hearts and red roses. A special something given to us by a boyfriend, a girlfriend, a wife, a husband, a lover, a friend, by a partner, or by a sweetheart.

A glitzy card, a dozen roses, a fancy dinner, perhaps some gourmet chocolates, even M & M's. Diamonds, jewelry, sexy lingerie, a stuffed bear. All symbols of love and affection. All saying, "I love you!" Hearts and flowers. The colors red and pink and purple painted on the front cover of a card. Love, hugs and passion. Cupid never had it so good!

Tiamo came into our household and our lives on the 10th of February. Just days before Valentine's Day. A day set aside for love. Romance. Passion. It's a day to express your feelings in more ways than just a quick "luv 'ya" as you hang up on the phone. It's a day to open up your heart to big hugs and love. A day to do more, show more and feel more.

When Tiamo first came into our lives, we had a hard time coming up with a name for her. We wanted something special, something indicative of her heritage but also of our love for each other.

Bernese Mountain Dogs originated from Switzerland and were named for the Canton of Bern. At one time, Bernese Mountain Dogs were a relatively rare breed. We wanted a name that honored her homeland and at the same time, represented our love.

We certainly weren't going to name her "Heidi," or "Daisy" or "Alppy." We scratched though a dozen or more names penciled on a list of possible dog names.

"Waggles" – might be a cute name for a puppy, but not so much for a mature canine.

"Lady" – not very original.

"Blackie" – again, no originality.

"Shasta" – Malcolm didn't like.

"Girl" – I didn't like. We were stumped.

Malcolm and I spent our honeymoon in Italy, a country seeped in love and romance. When we were in Bellagio, our hotel room looked out across Lake Como to the Swiss alps, miles away. In the mornings we were awakened by the church bells. In the late hours of the evening, we were awakened by thunder and lightening.

Throughout the beautiful days we would hop on a water taxi, crossing the narrow lake to the villages and villas scattered along the edges of the opposite shore. So we combined a little Swiss with a little Italian and came up with "Tiamo."

One look at our new puppy, with her four snow-capped paws and her white-tipped tail, so reminiscent of our view of the Alps, and we were in love. Totally smitten. She was a gift to

Malcolm for his 50th birthday, but she didn't arrive in Santa Fe until a few days before Valentine's Day. She was our love child.

Tiamo translates to 'I love you' in Italian. Each time we said her name, we were telling her we loved her. Just as every time her tail wagged, or she nose-nudged us for a quick ear scratch, she was sending us love. Returning the gift. It was our own special Valentine's Day gift, every day. All yearlong. We loved her deeply.

When we ended up with two of Tiamo's puppies, we were back in the same boat. We had a hard time finding names that "fit" our newest additions to the family.

To keep track of the litter, we identified our eight little ones by the color of the collar they wore. We had Butterfly, Pinkie, Cherry, Blackie, Burberry, Greenie, Apple and Little Butterfly. We certainly weren't going to continue calling our little girls, "Little Butterfly" and "Pinkie." New monikers were needed.

Once again, we racked our brains for befitting names. And, again, we crossed dozens of names off the list for various reasons. Some names were too long, too many syllables. Malcolm and I had already agreed on a three-syllable max. Some names were too silly. Some too common and over used. Some we just didn't like.

We looked up names on the internet. Hoping a perfect name would jump out at us. We watched the two little puppies as they played together, hoping their young emerging personalities would spark an idea. We came up blank. We were clueless.

"We could give them an Italian names," Malcolm commented.

"Like we did for Tiamo," he tacked on. We were both in agreement.

We started to throw out Italian names. "Bella," "Rosa," "Sophia." Once again, not very original. And, not names we particularly liked. Our pudgy little puppies didn't come close to looking like a "Sophia." In Malcolm's eyes, there was only one Sophia and she was a goddess on the movie screen. Still is a goddess for him. Sophia was not in the lineup.

"How about 'Dolce'?" I suggested. Malcolm rolled the name around on his tongue.

"Maybe," he allowed. Not ready to agree or disagree on the two-syllable name.

"We could call her 'Dolch' for short!" I optioned. That was a one-syllable alternative. I kind of liked the nickname. Immediately, I looked over to Little Butterfly and tried out the name.

"Here Dolce!," I called out to her. "Dolch!" I repeated as I shortened her name. Little Butterfly's ears perked up, her nose twitched and her little legs made quick work moving in my direction. Dolce had her new name.

"Now what about Pinkie?" Malcolm questioned. "Any ideas for her?"

"How about 'Diligo', meaning to hold in high esteem or prize, or 'Amore'?" I proposed. Amore was the Latin word for love.

"Might work." Malcolm agreed. He mulled over the names. Amore was at our maximum syllable range but still fit within our perimeters. Dolch was at the minimum.

In keeping with our Swiss/Italian theme, we ended up naming the girls, Dolce and Amore. Sweet and Love.

Dolce is sweet; a more gentle, kind dog you'll never find, she is our sweetheart. Evenings will find her curled up on my lap, snuggling against me. You'll see her tail thump every so often, her muzzle reaching up to lick my chin on occasion. Dog kisses. Her eyes softened by our touch, a look of contentment crossing her face. Dolce is our hugger, our snuggler, our little sweetheart. She is our own special Valentine's Day gift, every day. That girl gives more love than you could ever hold in your heart. Every day. So sweet.

Amore is love; a wild, crazy, passionate dog full of heart. She is the flip side of Dolce. With bright shinning eyes, Amore screams passion, and has given us an all-out, from the heart, love. Totally. She gives her all.

Amore is our Dennis the Menace. You can't help but chuckle over her antics. You can't help but love her. She is so full of life; every day with her is an adventure. We wake up each morning wondering what kinds of mischief will Amore get into today, what wild dog thing will she do. She radiates with happiness and exudes joy. She is our own special Valentine's Day gift, every day. Her unique gift to us is her love of life. She puts a big laugh in our hearts every day and places a huge smile in our souls. Every day.

Tiamo, Dolce, and Amore have given us more love than we could ever have imagined. They make our hearts smile and our souls sing. Every day. Not with flowers or chocolates or purple hearts. Not just on Valentine's Day but every day. Everyday of the year, they give us their hearts. Completely.

PUPPY BREATH

When told we were expecting our little litter of puppies, Celia, a dear and close friend exclaimed, "Ah, I so love puppy breath! It's so sweet" I thought she was plumb crazy. No dog had pleasant breath, let alone a puppy.

In the following weeks, several more friends and acquaintances made the same comment in varying degrees. We heard everything from, "puppy breath is so precious!" to "I just love their little breath!" to "their breath is adorable!"

Seriously? What planet are these people from? It's a dog's breath for gawds sake. I would politely smile, but under my own breath, I would mumble "good lawd" to Malcolm, who was trying in vain to keep a straight face.

It wasn't until the puppies were old enough to be held and played with that I started to get an inkling of what my friends meant. With their still pink little noses, at three-n-half weeks old, our little ones were just starting on softened puppy chow. They were old enough to be cuddled and held up close against our necks, while we absently rubbed their soft ears.

At five to six weeks, we were bringing our herd of yipping mutts outside to their playpen to enjoy the fresh air and the still warm fall days. Malcolm dragged a couple huge wooden rocking chairs into the pen so we could sit and watch the eight little blighters sniff and explore their new world. As they tired one by one, they would all end up at our feet, ready for a little puppy nap.

Inevitably, I would end up with two or three canine belly balls in my lap, falling fast asleep in my arms, their fat round tummies gently swaying with their soft breathing. I would stay put, not daring to move. I didn't want to disturb their sleep, enjoying their little bodies snuggled up in my lap and arms.

On warm sunny days, Malcolm and I would sit in the pen for hours, enjoying the melodious sounds coming from the puppies. Loving the feel of their silky fur, their soft little paws pressed against our arms, their muzzle tucked under our chins. It was during these endearing moments, that I learned the true meaning of "puppy breath."

Truth be told, there is something sweet about little puppy's breath! The scent is precious, with just a hint of baby puppy. Celia was right.

Taking a deep breath, I smell a little puppy's trust, I inhale the wonders and joys of a pint-sized creature filled with faith in their human caretakers. I breathe in the love of a new friend and the loyalty of an old one. I catch a whiff of an adoring puppy, a devoted dog, a committed canine to its custodian.

Now when I hear those same "I just love puppy breath," I totally get it. Puppy breath is a precious bouquet of entrusting love.

SIMPLY IRRESISTIBLE

As puppies, Amore and Dolce were simply irresistible. Loveable and adorable. Sweet and charming and delightful and gorgeous. They were puppy cute! And they knew it!

The problem is, they still are irresistible! It's hard to resist two beautiful dogs. And they know it! Boy, do they know it!

As puppies, they were the sweetest, cutest little things. With their little white-tipped tails wagging to and fro, their noses wrinkling as they sniffed out new territory, their puppy breath as they pressed puppy kisses on our faces. They were adorable. Between their roly-poly tummies and their short, little stubby legs, they were absolutely lovable. Malcolm and I never stood a chance!

I think that was one reason how we ended up with two puppies instead of one. It's pretty hard to resist adorable puppies. It's damn near impossible to resist a Berner puppy.

Amore and Dolce each have their particular quirks which only endears them to us even more.

Dolce will tilt her head as she learns a new command. You can almost see the wheels turning as she tries to figure out the process, her brain working out the equation. She is our thinker.

Of the two, Dolce learned her lessons quick and fast. She also learned she would be rewarded with a treat if she scored high marks for her quest. After she accomplishes her task, Dolce will sit at our feet, tilting her head to the side, patiently waiting for her gold star, her reward, her treat. She trusts us to deliver our promise.

Again, you can follow Dolce's thought process: perform her task, receive her treat. Upon completion of her mission, her brain starts to analyze where her special nibble might be, and when would she be getting it. How could anyone resist such an appealing sight? Dolce brings smiles to our hearts with just a tilt of her head.

If Dolce was in high school, she would be the honors student, the one who never got in trouble, never cussed, smoked or slept around. Didn't drink and was home before curfew. A regular little Miss Goody-Two-Shoes. The Teacher's pet. Always currying favor and pretty hard to resist.

Now, Amore on the other hand, will raise a brown-winged eyebrow, as if to question our sanity in asking her to perform the small learning task.

"You want me to do what?" she will silently sass, looking at us askew, head tilted to be sure she understood us correctly.

"Seriously? Again? How many times do I have to do this?" she'll question, she is done playing games. She wants the treat, but not to rehearse her training. She would much rather run after a lizard than be stuck practicing her cues. Training be dammed, being a brat is much more fun than being a well behaved, well-mannered canine.

"Just give me my treat!" Amore insists. Nudging us with her muzzle.

First her ears would flick back and forth, then her two matching red-brown brows would draw together, frowning, not sure she wants to do as asked. With a puppy pout and long drawn-out sigh, her eyebrows would twitch up and down once more before she grudgingly follows the command. She wants that treat more than she is willing to admit!

Amore makes us laugh. And giggle. And chuckle. And chortle. And she brings us such joy. She is our canine jokester. She wants the treat, but she doesn't want to work for it.

If Amore could speak to us, she would try to talk her way out of practicing her manners. She doesn't have time for such nonsense. She lives life in the fast lane and isn't planning on slowing down one bit. Amore's allure is in her personality.

If Amore was a teenager, she would be the rebellious 16-year-old, stealing a smoke behind the gym bleachers, swigging Jimmy B out of a paper bag. The horror student. The badass belligerent punk rebelling against authority. The one everyone secretly admires. Sweet only on Sundays.

Between Dolce's head tilt and Amore's brow lift, Malcolm and I have never stood a chance. One forty-five degree slant of the head and a five-degree raise of the brow has us wrapped around every one of their paws.

The two of them are simply irresistible. It's been that way ever since they were born. Every day.

Megan McFarlane

COUNTER SURFING

Tiamo was taught early on not to beg. We were especially carefully not to feed her our table scraps or human food. She knew the rules and she obeyed them, or so we thought....

We learned to our dismay, as soon as we left the room or our backs were turned, mischief happened. Leave something tasty on the counter and she'd be waiting in the wings ready for a counter-attack.

Tiamo had an alarmingly keen sense of timing, along with a keen sense of balance, so specialized and perfected, she could lift a whole loaf of pumpkin bread off the counter without dropping a crumb. And she'd be out the dog door before you returned. She could transport a filled glass coffee creamer 20 yards to the doggy door and out to the pen without spilling a drop of evidence or breaking the glass.

Her specialty was cookies. Since she only took one, most times I didn't realize there was one less of a dozen. And, if I suspected a thief, all I had to do was look to my husband – a likely culprit.

Tiamo was wise. She knew not to look suspicious or culpable. No guilty look, no "if-I-can't-see-you-you-can't-see-me" covering of the eyes, no hiding in the corner. She was smart. She was sly. She was cunning. Boy, did she had cunning down to a fine art. She hid her crimes in the open. Or, if she knew she might get busted, she would lay down on the goods, hiding them under her fur lined belly and poise innocently, her paws delicately crossed. "Who me?" her eyes asked, her demeanor innocent. Yes, she was that good.

Her Oscar performances usually led me to scold Amore and Dolce and on occasion, Malcolm. Oh, she was good! So good, she knew to paw the canisters on the counter back into position after shoving them out of the way to grab the tasty treasure hidden behind. We learned not to thaw out steaks on the counter, leave bread out or wait to wash the dishes until later. Later meant the dinner menu needed to be changed.

A while back, I had asked Malcolm to pull out some hamburger from the freezer to thaw for dinner. He placed the meat towards the back of the counter well out of reach from sniffing noses and searching paws. Unfortunately, he forgot to move the step stool used to reach for items on the top shelf in the cabinets.

No surprise here. Tiamo had climbed on the stool and was licking the thawing hamburger. When she realized she was busted, she grabbed the still slightly frozen block of meat in her jaws and ran through the house and out into the dog pen. By the time, we had gone around to the pen she had gulped down the hamburger and was licking off the leftovers, the protective paper wrapper in shreds.

We often have friends over for an evening meal. Especially in the summer months. Our summer evenings usually are a wonderful temperature to host outside dinners under our back portal. Malcolm will grill while the rest of us relax near by on overstuffed chairs on the back patio.

On one such evening, Malcolm brought a platter of boneless chicken breasts inside to the kitchen counter to "rest" while we continued to finish our drinks before starting dinner. Always careful with Tiamo around, he covered the platter with foil and pushed it to the back of the counter.

A few minutes later, with the back door open, I heard a little clink, clink from inside. "Clink," I heard again. I was puzzled. I heard another little clink. It was just faint enough, Malcolm didn't even hear it, nor our guests. Another clink.

"Son-of-a-bitch!" I yelled. It took me 15 seconds to decipher the sound. I sprinted into the house. Tiamo had found the platter with chicken. She had grabbed the platter with her mouth and had lifted it down from the counter to the floor. The clinks I was hearing were the platter hitting the counter and again on the floor. By the time I had run into the house, the chicken was devoured, the plate empty.

Tiamo's favorite stolen prize off the counter was freshly made Pumpkin Bread. Time and time again, she found ways to snarf the loaf I just baked and had cooling on the counter. It got to the point where we had to store the cooling loafs in the microwave above the stove just to avoid bite marks out of the middle.

An empty and cold dishwasher is another great cooling rack as well as a cold oven. I'm just telling ya' some of the hiding places we have had to use and implement. Don't use the sink, a large dog can reach in its depths if determined enough!

Tiamo was our counter-surfing thief. Using her nose, she first raised her muzzle, moving slowly along the perimeter of the kitchen, sniffing around the edges of the counters. When she located a scent worthy of investigating, her front paws would be the first line of attack. Up they went, landing on the counter tops.

Paws on the counter, Tiamo was in position to scan the battlefield. Head high enough to scout for possible edible goodies, she could eye the counter tops for treats, sweets, and meats. She would balance against the counters with her big paws and dance her way around the kitchen until she found the perfect bite. BINGO! The prize was spotted!

Tiamo was crafty. She knew she didn't want to be caught, as that literately meant being the dog house. She would contemplate both Malcolm's and my locations. Looking left and right, she explored the open living/dining room. She listened for where in the house we might be at. Laundry room? Den? Outside? Her ears twitched, taking note of where we might be, ready to move.

When the coast was clear, when she felt we were otherwise occupied, when she knew it was safe, she made her move. Front paw extended, she could reach across the counter. Pawing the desired treat towards the front of the counter, Tiamo maneuvered the treasured booty within grasp. Her mighty jaws locked around the ill-gotten gains. Victory was close. Retreating to the pen was her next move.

"TIAMO!" vibrated through the house. I looked up from what I was doing in another room. What the hell? I held my breath, waiting to see if I was needed. Waiting to hear more.

"DROP!" I heard Malcolm's command coming from the kitchen area. Malcolm's deep voice could be heard over the radio I had playing in the laundry room as I folded clothes. I peeked around the corner to see what Tiamo had done now.

"TIAMO! DROP!" Malcolm firmly restated. I entered the kitchen just as Tiamo dropped her head, but not her treasure, the food still clamped in her jaws. Her eyes shifted to me, was I going to be her enemy or her champion? Would I let her keep her prize or would I take it from her? I watched Tiamo mentally weigh her options.

Tiamo had snagged a good sized block of Cheddar Cheese left out from Malcolm's sandwich makings for lunch. Not just any kind of cheese, but Hilmar Cheese Company Cheddar Cheese. Shipped only in the cold months, Malcolm coveted HCC cheese.

Even I am told not to eat the favored HCC cheese, but to use the "other" stuff. HCC cheese was his, and there was a limited supply. Tiamo had grabbed the HCC cheese. She was messing with the good stuff.

Tiamo had hit the jackpot of all counter-surfing winnings when she seized that block of cheese. She was not about to let it go. For a dog, cheese is a mighty incentive to being naughty. There was no regret, no pang of guilt for her actions. No remorse, no shame. It was left out on the counter, therefore she considered it fair-game. In her eyes, the cheese was hers.

I watched Tiamo's eyes go from a dull disappointment in being busted, caught in the act of counter-surfing stealth to brightening into a wicked gleam. Tiamo had a plan. There was no time to warn Malcolm. Tiamo was not about to give up her loot.

Tiamo saw her chance. As Malcolm bent forward to physically remove the cheese from Tiamo's tightly clinched muzzle, Tiamo dashed through his wide leg stance. Straight through his denim covered legs, the opening just wide enough for her to push through the gap. The momentum from Tiamo's rushing pushed Malcolm off balance, tipping him over and landing him hard on his arse on the brick floor.

"Oomph!" exploded from Malcolm's lungs. Time stood still. I waited to see what Malcolm would do.

After a shocked moment, Malcolm belted out, "Well don't just stand there! Help me up!" I couldn't help but chortle. He lay sprawled out on the middle of the kitchen floor, on his back, his feet up in the air. Chuckling under my breath, I extended a hand to pull him to an upright position.

I caught Malcolm's eye and saw a little twinkle flicker and catch hold. Laughter erupted. We stood there laughing so hard we were bent over, tears in our eyes. It took us a full five minutes to recover from laughing.

Tiamo had made her move and it was a good one. If she was going to be in trouble, it was going to be worth her while. Full guns.

Running on full throttle, Tiamo headed for the pen. She was the victor over the cheese turf war. By the time we had recovered from our laughter, the coveted Hilmar Cheese Company cheese was gulped down and consumed, the wrapper was ripped and torn and left behind in the weeds.

Malcolm learned to clean up after himself!

CURFEW

Prior to Tiamo, we had Thugs. A cat. A big ol' barn cat given to me by a college friend. Named Thugs because he was the bully of the litter, he had black tuffs on his ears like a bobcat and beautiful green eyes. He easily looked like a lynx or a bobcat, although smaller. He sported gray, white and black swirls on his sides and stripes on his tail. He was a cat that was king of his domain and by gawd, he knew it. Thugs was an unusual and unique cat.

Thugs was one of those types of cats everyone loved, everyone admired, and everyone remembered. Born into a wild barn cat litter, Thugs was the "tyrant" of the bunch. He was a little thug in the true sense of the word. As a kitten, he would torment his siblings, pouncing on his littermates, playing rough and acting tough. As an adult feline, he would sit on his perch and give us humans a look of pure disdain, dismissing us with a flick of his tail.

Thugs was a great mouser and lizard chaser. Man, that boy could hunt! We would find remnants of his safaris on our front door step. He kept our house mouse free and lizard clean.

He tolerated being picked up but loved being petted. He would sit by the front door to be let outside, emitting a loud meow in his impatience if we were too slow in our response time. Then softly tap on the window screen when he was ready to come back inside.

"Tap tap, tap tap tap tap," we would hear. Looking over to the window, we would see Thugs' front paws banging on the window screen. Like drum sticks tapping on a drum, there was a cadence to his signal. "Let me in!" his determined big paws tapped.

"Thugs wants in," Malcolm relayed to me as he was spread out on the couch reading the paper.

"You let him in," I replied back, "you're closer!"

"But he will want to sit on me once he's inside so I need to be in position," Malcolm bantered back, not moving so much as an inch off the sofa.

"Pffft!" as I walked over to the back door to let our big ol' Thugs back inside through the slider. Malcolm was right. Thugs would leap up on the couch onto Malcolm's belly, twirl around a few times looking for the best position and lay down on Malcolm's torso, promptly taking a little cat nap.

He mellowed as he aged, loved to sit on Malcolm's firm six-pack abs (hee hee) as Malcolm read the New York Times on the sofa. Thugs would send a perturbed look Malcolm's way when Malcolm needed to change positions or rise from the couch. Thugs did not like to be interrupted.

Cold mornings would find him curled up on our down pillows next to our heads, basking in the comfort of the blanket's warmth. In the evenings he would follow us from room to room waiting for us to go to bed. Thugs still patrolled his home turf, keeping the varmints to a minimum. He still wanted in and out of his castle as he secured his kingdom.

Thugs was already 15 years old when we migrated to the State of New Mexico, land of bobcats, coyotes, snakes, and cactus.

Most felines in New Mexico don't live much longer than a few years, especially if they sneak outdoors when the back door is opened. Cats are at the bottom of the food chain in New Mexico. Low man on the totem pole. And here was Thugs, at age fifteen, an old cat in most eyes. We had our work cut out for us to keep him healthy and alive.

Thugs had already outlived his life expectancy by New Mexico's standards by many, many years and now he was firmly sitting on the lowest tier of the animal kingdom hierarchy. We knew we needed to be careful. We lived outside of the city limits where coyotes are a common sighting. Keeping Thugs safe was our priority.

Felines in New Mexico are often a tasty meal for coyotes. Large falcons and eagles can easily sink their talons into the soft fur of a cat. There were many dangers just lurking around the bush, waiting in prey for an unsuspecting cat. Luckily, Thugs was savvy and smart and stayed safe, plus we imposed a strict curfew.

Malcolm and I incorporated the 10 and 4 rule. Thugs was only allowed outside between 10 a.m. and 4 p.m. No earlier, no later. Thugs had been born an outdoor cat. Born in a barn, he was used to roaming, preying on his hunt, only coming indoors in the evenings. He was used to being outside, used to coming and going as he wished. It was hard to place restrictions on him.

Back in our old hometown, Thugs had been safe in the wild outdoors of suburbia, where nature was kind to him. Not so much in New Mexico. We counted our blessings he liked to stay close to the house and napped on a lounge cushion under the back portal, where he was relatively protected. Keeping Thugs only indoors would have been torture for him and for us.

Thugs wasn't too happy with us when we brought Tiamo into the family. He let Tiamo know real quick who was the boss with sharp claws to Tiamo's curious nose within five minutes of being introduced. Tiamo learned to keep her distance and in the beginning of their relationship, wouldn't come into the room if Thugs was already there.

Tiamo would sit in the doorway, waiting for Thugs to move far enough away for her to safely enter. If Thugs was on the couch, Tiamo would give him a wide berth, measuring the distance between her nose and Thugs' claws.

Once Thugs trapped Tiamo in the utility room. Laying down in the middle of the entryway, Thugs calmly cleaned himself, while Tiamo nervously tried to figure out how to get around him and out of the room. Tiamo stayed in the utility room for over an hour, waiting to be released.

Within three months, the two of them were inseparable. Where Thugs went, Tiamo followed. Keeping her distance, Tiamo would trail and shadow Thugs around the perimeter of the house. When Thugs was ready for his afternoon snooze on the portal, jumping up on a soft outdoor chair pad, Tiamo would lay on the bricks along the side of the chair calmly waiting for the next move.

By five months, Thugs was strolling underneath Tiamo's belly and at nine months we would find them curled up together, Thugs gently purring, Tiamo emitting soft snores as they lay sleeping side by side. When they both were on the bed, Thugs would knead Tiamo until one of them would tire of the motion and jump off. They were devoted friends and would be to their dying days.

Thugs was one of those cats that aged well. After 17 years, he was still going strong, although much slower. He had some hearing loss, and his vision was less clear, but all in all he was hale and healthy.

Over the course of a year, Tiamo became his protector. If Thugs was outside, Tiamo tracked his moves, following Thugs through the junipers and chamisa, keeping tabs on his whereabouts. When Thug's four o'clock curfew hit, we would call

Tiamo to "go get Thugs." Tiamo would round-up Thugs and herd him back into the house.

"Find Thugs" was one of Tiamo's favorite games. Come close to curfew time and Tiamo would be sitting by the door, tail wagging, eagerly waiting to go "Find Thugs."

It was also one of Thugs favored pastimes. Loving to antagonize Tiamo, Thugs would sit up high on a tree branch waiting for Tiamo to come find him. He would flick his tail while balancing on the limb, benignly perusing his world as seen from a juniper limb.

Tiamo would sit at the base of the tree, impatiently waiting for Thugs to jump off his perch and meander into the house. Close on his heels, Tiamo was at the ready to gently guide Thugs into the warm and safe haven of the living room. The two of them would make their way through the back door, Thugs first, Tiamo respectively following.

When Thugs was 19 years old, he was too old to be let outside. Thugs was showing his age and he was slowing down. His movements were stiff, his leaps not as high. Thugs slept most of the time, curled up in the sun's warmth as it shined through our huge living room picture windows.

Thugs would amble through the house, searching out Tiamo to curl up against. He could still jump up on the bed, kneading Tiamo's belly at night time, but Thugs' rough and rumble life was taking a toll on him. His hunting days were over.

Twenty-one years old and our little bully was old and tired. Eating less, losing weight, Thug's curfew was up. Tiamo's game of "Find Thugs" was in the final quarter. It was fourth and ten and time to punt. Thugs was ready to go to his next life and Tiamo knew. She knew and was already prepared for missing her friend.

We buried Thugs in our Memorial Garden where other beloved pets are laid to rest, under the branches of his juniper tree, where he would wait for Tiamo to come find him.

Later, we would often find Tiamo in the garden, eyes full of sorrow, laying next to where we buried Thugs, her head resting over the disturbed dirt. We all missed Thugs but especially Tiamo. She missed her friend. She missed curling up together for an afternoon nap. She missed Thugs kneading her at night time before they went to bed. She missed Thugs.

It was amazing that Thugs lived to the ripe ol' age of almost twenty-two years. Twenty-two amazing years, but then, Thugs was an amazing cat and Tiamo and Thugs had an amazing friendship.

We should all be so fortunate as to have a companion to knead.

OUR PAPER BOY

I'm of the belief that canines, especially those breeds that belong to the Working Dog Group, need to feel important. They need to know they have a valuable function within the family dynamics, a job to perform that is essential to their caretakers.

Dogs such as the Bernese Mountain Dog, were bred to pull small farm carts loaded down with heavy milk cans for the dairies. Their deep barreled chest made them an ideal breed to work on a farm, driving goat herds to and from their pastures and drafting farm supplies from the villages. While we don't have a dairy for the girls to work in, I have tried to find appropriate chores for them to perform to feel useful.

On that note, I looked no further than our own paper box.

Tiamo was barely a year old when she first started to fetch the daily newspaper. At first she would just walk up the long drive with me to get the morning paper. She would prance her way up the driveway, excitement shining in her eyes, hoping for a glimpse of a cottontail or a low flying bird she could chase.

I'd call her back, reprimanding her for leaving my side. She'd hang her head, giving me her sorrowful look that was just shy of asking for forgiveness and pretend to be good for the rest of the walk to the paper.

With the misbegotten belief that she was exonerated for misbehaving earlier, Tiamo would try to play the "grab the paper and run" game on the return trip back to the house.

I had a habit of tucking the rolled up newspaper under my arm, leaving my hands free, usually in my coat pockets to keep warm. Thinking of the paper as the golden prize to be had, Tiamo would jump high to nip at the paper under my arm, hoping to grab it and sprint her way to triumph. She recognized my hands were otherwise occupied, staying warm beneath the folds of my jacket. She knew she had the advantage and she took it.

On the days Tiamo was able to lock onto the paper, grabbing it from under my arm, she would run a victory lap around the house, many times dropping her precious paper somewhere in the back forty. I would have to go search for the paper under wet, dew soaked tumbleweeds and stickers, stumbling over gopher mounds and mice holes – not so much fun at six o'clock in the morning.

I knew I had to teach her respect for the printed word soon or we would have shredded bits of paper throughout our property as she tore into her prize.

And so her training began…..

Our paper usually arrived wrapped in a plastic sleeve to protect it from the elements. I figured the blue plastic baggie would also shield the paper from Tiamo's drool, if I could just teach her to carry the paper back to the house.

Using a leash to keep her close and her favorite treats to reward her, I trained Tiamo to carry our newspaper from the paper box situated at the end of the drive across the street, down to the house and drop it on the floor by the couch. It took one week.

She had such a gentle mouth, she never tore the plastic protective covering, keeping the rolled paper pristine. After a successful month of transporting our paper, I started unleashing her. Tiamo never once strayed away from my side. Fun and games was over, she knew she had an important job to do. She had a role to perform. She was all business.

A few more weeks of free range paper hauling and I taught her to reach into the bright yellow paper box, pulling out the newspaper by herself. I would open the box flap and Tiamo would reach in to grab the paper. Within a month, Tiamo could nose the plastic flap open and grasp the rolled paper in her muzzle. She no longer needed my assistance.

From here on out, I was no longer allowed to remove the paper from the plastic holder – that was Tiamo's responsibility. Her job. Doing so would result in a barking frenzy and a strong nose nudge under my arm to release the paper. I was forever banned from getting the paper, nobody was going to do Tiamo's job.

It didn't take long before I didn't even have to walk up the driveway with Tiamo. I'd let Tiamo out the front gate of the portal and stay behind, keeping an eye on her as she ran up the drive, grab the newspaper from the box and jog back down to me. The paper gently clutched between her jaws, pride sparkling in her eyes.

Tiamo kept her job, even after her litter was born and Dolce and Amore became part of our household. That was her task. Her job. Tiamo never allowed Dolce and Amore to be a part of her paper route. It was our special time. Tiamo's and mine. It was her duty. I'd let her out the front portal gate and she would dash up the driveway to grab the morning news. Dolce and Amore still in the house.

Reading the newspaper with a strong cup of coffee seems to go hand in hand, and Malcolm is a pro at both. Reading the paper from stem to stern and drinking his coffee. Tiamo would bring in the paper from outside and drop the rolled up rubber banded news at his feet. Mission accomplished. Job done.

As Malcolm sipped and read the various sections of the paper, Tiamo would lay beside him on her Kilim covered ottoman for her morning snooze. She had done her job and was ready for her nap.

I never tried to teach Dolce and Amore to fetch the paper – I always considered that Tiamo's duty. It has always been Tiamo's job and a chore we shared. Besides, I know for a fact, Dolce and Amore would have fought big time over who got to carry the newspaper, resulting in shredded newspaper up and down the driveway.

With Tiamo's passing, I walk the drive alone, grabbing the morning paper out of the now-weathered yellow paper box. I'm back to tucking the rolled news up under my arm, keeping my hands warm in my pockets.

Sweet memories of Tiamo attempting to snatch the paper out from my control often come to mind.

I miss our morning ritual – now a-days, the paper just doesn't read the same.

FRIDAY NIGHTS

Friday. 5:00 p.m. Time to close up shop. Time to head on out. Time to shut down the computer, turn off the copier and printer. Time to head home to the hubby and the dogs and start the weekend. I work for a state trade association for REALTORS® where it's easy to get hung up from leaving for the day. A phone call right at the critical hour is all it takes. Right at 5:00 p.m. Right when I'm calling it quits for the day.

About two years after we had our litter of puppies, on a late Friday afternoon in early summer, I was doing exactly that. Shutting off lights and grabbing my keys to head out the door from work, when the phone rang. Right when I was leaving for home. It was 5:02 p.m.

A distraught Association member was on the line, frantic that their entire brokerage was unable to access their internet-based real estate forms library. To a REALTOR® this is bad - really bad - especially with the weekend looming in the background. Our members work holidays. They work weekends. They work after closing time. I needed to get them back in business.

This particular Brokerage was one of our largest firms. I had over 200 REALTORS® twittering their thumbs impatiently waiting to get back to business. Their busiest day of the week was only 15 hours away.

I dropped back down into my office chair with a deep sigh and began damage control. Multiple phone calls to our vendor back east, several phone calls to my contact at the brokerage. It was another two hours later before I was able to correct their "user" error.

In the middle of their crisis, I phoned home to let Malcolm know I'd be late and to hold off on dinner. It had been a long week just made longer, but I was able to keep 200 real estate brokers in business for the weekend. Weary and tired, I locked up the office and headed home.

About an half-hour later, I walked in our front door. I was tired, hungry and grouchy. Really grouchy! And there was my sweet, wonderful husband, (did I place enough emphasis on the sweet and wonderful part?) waiting for me at the door, a blended margarita with salt on the rim of the glass in one hand, the dogs eagerly awaiting to be allowed to hug me with their welcome home attack being held back with the other. A platter of appetizers (okay, it was just cheese and salami with salsa but he is still wonderful!) was sitting on the kitchen counter.

Malcolm grabbed my purse and handed me my drink with orders to go outside and sit on the wicker lounger on the portal.

"Kick off your heels, put something comfortable on and I'll meet you outside on the portal," he commanded. I was more than happy to comply.

The shoes went flying, my skirt dropped to the bedroom floor as I walked into the closet to grab some sweats. I headed to the back portal, the dogs at my heels. They waited just longed enough for me to get comfortable.

Once settled, Dolce immediately crawled up on the long padded outdoor chaise and curled up between my legs, putting her head on my lap. How did she know I needed a little canine love? That I needed a dog hug?

Tiamo sat down by my side, getting her ears gently rubbed as I sipped my Margarita. Amore, never one to sit still, moseyed over for a quick back rub then went off searching for lizards, stopping back through periodically for more rubs. I had my girls (mostly) by my side and I had my man. Like the ice in my margarita, the day's worries slowly melted away.

Malcolm and I slowly caught up on the week's happenings as I unwound from my long and horrid workday. Normally I love my work, but this Friday went to hell in a hand basket as soon as I walked in the office. I was glad to be home, glad it was the weekend. I breathed in the deep outdoor scents, the junipers, the pinon, the cacti. I was home with my husband and my girls, watching the sunset, drinking margaritas. The stress slid away from my shoulders.

One sip led to an empty glass. The first margarita led to two more drinks. The cheese and salami platter ended up being our dinner as we watched the sun settle down behind the Sandia Mountain Range. While the tension eased and I was able to relax, the dogs stayed by my side. Dolce still in my lap, Tiamo still getting her ears scratched. Amore swinging by every 10 minutes or so for a little attention. Malcolm and I continued to exchange comments and conversation, sipping through our drinks, snacking on the cheese and crackers.

Dolce never lifted her head from my lap, content to be on top of me. Tiamo never left my side. Amore would amble over every so often throughout the night ensuring all was well. Malcolm and I talked until well after all the stars were lit up and sparkling. It was late in the evening before we came inside for the evening. It was one of the best nights ever and the start of our "Friday night - wine night."

The following Friday, I was able to head out for the weekend without any phone calls or delays. Five o-clock on the dot, I was on my way home from work.

I called Malcolm, "hey Hon, why don't you uncork a bottle of red and pour two glasses. I'll be home soon," I requested.

"Already done!" he answered. He must of read my mind.

"Are you going to want dinner later or will cheese and crackers be enough?" he questioned.

"Just nibbles," I wasn't in the mood for a heavy meal. The previous Friday night was so perfect, I wanted to replicate it.

Summers in Santa Fe are gorgeous, absolutely spectacular. It's our monsoon season. The afternoon rain showers that cool down the day's heat, create some stunning sunsets. The leftover clouds light up with brilliant gold, orange and red hues as the sky opens its doors to the evening night.

By the time I arrived home, Malcolm had put together another tray of hors d'oeuvres, two glasses filled with an Australian Malbec were waiting on the counter. Breathing. Some soft piano jazz music was quietly being infused throughout the house. The mood was set. Another perfect evening.

We sat outside on the portal, the dogs once again at our feet, content in hearing our voices as we conversed, sipping on our wine. Nibbling on the tray of treats. Every once in awhile I would slip Tiamo a slice of cheddar cheese when Malcolm wasn't watching. Amore would still periodically check in with us. Dolce stayed curled up next to me on the chaise. My family was gathered close.

We have continued our Friday night wine nights ever since. On occasion we invite friends and neighbors over to join us, but mostly it just the girls and the two us. On cold winter nights we stay inside, Malcolm lighting a fire while we enjoy a warm toddy, Dolce always by my side. Tiamo at my feet. Amore, always restless, swinging through every so often.

Sometimes our wine night is a simple affair. Sometimes I'm traveling and it's skipped over. Sometimes we don't have much to say in conversation. Sometimes we talk until midnight. Sometimes we just sit in the quiet with the dogs. And sometimes we pick up our books, reading in shared company.

Malcolm will change up the menu of appetizers and beverages. He will pour a crisp white wine in the summers and a hearty red in the winter. He'll go on a Sangria bent for a few weeks in a row, adding different ingredients to give the drink some complexity until he gets it just right. Then he will mix up a pitcher of Margaritas when the weather is warm and make his own style of New Mexican Salsa. Straight out of a jar. He will offer up a "Malcolm concoction." Who knows what's been added and stirred in but it's tasty. Through it all, I call our Friday nights our "Wine Night."

Inevitably, co-workers and members will often ask about "wha'cha doin' for the weekend?"

"Any plans?" they will inquire as we are heading out of the office at closing time, locking up the office for the weekend.

"Wine night tonight," is my standard response. Wine night has become my favorite night of the week. My beacon when it's a been a rough week. My encouragement. Sleeping in on weekends is no longer the highlight of the weekend. My anticipation for the weekend starts with our "Wine Night."

If we happen to have company in town for the weekend, "Wine Night" is what is served for Friday's night dinner. Consequently, "Wine Night" has become a favorite among our guests. Many times, they will bring the wine and some snacks to add to our evening.

Since Tiamo's passing, Amore has taken to laying down at my feet, keeping them warm, letting me know she is right there. She'll lift her head when she hears a car drive by, check out what's happening when Malcolm gets up to add another log on the fire and come right back to me, leaning up against my feet. Eventually, she'll roll over and fall asleep. She'll start to snore, relaxed and at ease. Her family close by, safe.

Dolce still likes to stay put somewhere close to my lap. Her front paws touching my leg, her head usually leaning against me. Dolce has always been my lapdog. She is content.

I believe the girls enjoy the evenings as much as Malcolm and I do. I believe they hear the cadence of our voices, the low tones of our words and know their pack, their family is all right.

All's well in their world.

WELCOME HOME ATTACK

My job requires some travel, mostly around the state, but on occasion, I attend industry conferences that cross state lines. Every August/September, I attend our state association's annual Fall Conference. While the location of the conference is usually only an hour away from Santa Fe, I still need to stay at the conference hotel for a few nights.

My wonderful hubby will stay home with the dogs on most of my travel trips, saving us a lot of $$$$ in boarding costs and subsequent vet bills from coughs and other ailments the girls pick up at the doggy hotel. When travel includes a trip to a "cool" city or location, Malcolm will tag along, enjoying the sights while I'm in meetings.

This conference trip was a get-away from dog hair and dogs in the bed. Malcolm elected to stay home with the girls as I would only be in Albuquerque, just a short sixty mile stretch down the Interstate from Santa Fe.

It is pure joy being able to stretch across the king-sized bed with crisp, fresh, high thread count sheets and sink-your-head onto soft downy pillows. But, as much as I love having the bed to myself, I still miss my girls! (and my husband!). I usually call home checking to see how they are.

It so happened that on this trip, we received some rain while I was away. Those wet drops from heaven are a rare event in our drought stricken state of New Mexico. We live among dirt roads that quickly turn into slick mud with just the slightest presence of moisture. Ooey, gooey, slippery clay-mud roads. The slip and slide type of dirt roads.

We don't usually walk the dogs when it's raining or if the roads are muddy. Not only because of the mess from the mud and muck, but also because of our arid landscape and our many arroyos, flash flooding from the rain's surface water is common and very dangerous.

The torrential flood waters come down from higher ground, usually starting as a trickle and turning into a roaring river within seconds, crashing through junipers, chamisa and cacti. We just don't take the risk of getting caught in a flash flood. Consequently, the girls didn't get their walk for three days while I was out-of-town.

The first day away, I called Malcolm, checking to see how the girls were doing. Malcolm reported that from 4:30 to 7:00 p.m. all three dogs waited by the window, lined up shoulder to shoulder, looking and waiting for my car to pull into the driveway after work. Up until 10:00 p.m. they went tearing through the house every time they heard a car drive by, thinking it might be me returning home.

"They miss you," he murmured on the phone. His southern accent poking through on the line due to the lateness of the night.

"Ah, I miss them too," I cooed back, conveniently forgetting the extra legroom in the bed with the clean sheets sans dog hair.

Day two was much the same but with more grit and a lot more edge. There was still a drizzling rain, making the trails miserable to navigate. Walking in the mud is no fun. You slip, you slide, you fall. Your boots stick in the mire and lift off your foot. It's extremely taxing and tiring. You use leg muscles you didn't even know you had as you traverse the clay bog.

Malcolm calls just as I'm getting back to my room.

"When you getting home? The natives are getting restless. Haven't been able to walk the girls due to the rain," He greeted me. No hello, how-ya-doing, how was your day. I picked up on his silent S.O.S.

It had been just under 48 hours since the girls' last walk, their human mom still not home and the peanut butter Kongs are outside in the pouring rain. Dolce is bored and Amore has way too much energy bundled inside her 100 lb. frame. Tiamo is being Tiamo. Malcolm is starting to go nuts from dealing with the three dogs 24/7. Wet dog smell is permeating the house from the dogs racing back and forth from the dog pen to the house, tracking in mud and dirt. And Malcolm still has another day to live through.

"Tomorrow around 5:00 p.m. or so," I comment. "Maybe 6:00ish," I tacked on, just in case I was going to be late. I was only gone for three days.

"Well, come straight home!" he barked. Malcolm doesn't usually complain. He loves the dogs and enjoys his time with them. It was unusual to hear him growl, but it was obvious, he had had enough. Enough of the dogs without a walk. Enough of the mud. Just enough. He had hit his tether and was done. "Poke a fork in it" done.

By the third day, Amore wants company and wants to be entertained. Starting in the early hours of the morning. She has a bad habit of whacking her tail against the wall by the headboard when she comes to the side of the bed, checking to see if anyone has risen yet. On this day, she started her tail whacking at 3:30 a.m. trying to wake Malcolm up. She was bored. Bored and missing mom. Bored and wanted attention. Get-in-trouble bored.

She barked at every car that drove by and resorted to jumping on and off the bed desperately wanting Malcolm to get up. There is no rest for the wicked, Malcolm still has to live through another ten hours into the evening before I'll be home.

I dialed his cell. "I'm on my way! Be home in about an hour or so," I reported.

"You okay?" I asked.

"No!" He said tiredly. "I haven't had any sleep!" He was definitely grouchy.

"Grrrrr! Amore started with her tail whacking at 3:30 a.m. this morning. I haven't had any sleep since then. They are all yours when you get home!" he warned.

While the rain had abated to a light sprinkle – the roads were still muddy. This was to be the third day in a row the dogs had gone without a walk. Malcolm hadn't talked to an adult in three days, a full 72 hours, and wanted only to sip his Mexican Coca-Cola with pure cane sugar and read the newspaper in peace, i.e., no dogs, no wife. Still in my business attire, I arrive home early evening.

Tiamo, Amore and Dolce heard my car turn slowly down the gravel driveway and immediately started to bark, the clamor alerting Malcolm to the possibility of my return. The three of them race to the door to the garage, wanting out to greet me.

Immediately, Malcolm turned into the stereotyped housewife who hands the baby over to dad as he walks into the house from a hard day's work. He'd had enough of the dogs and it was going to be my turn to deal with them. It didn't matter that I was bringing home the bacon. The girls were going to be my responsibility.

He clicked open the garage door, letting all three, one hundred pound super-charged, super-hyper canines who haven't had a walk in three days, out to greet me. The race to be the first one to receive love from mom was on. I'm so busy dealing with the three dogs, I don't even notice Malcolm heading back into the house.

I received the welcome home attack from our girls!

Dolce was first to reach me. She literally leaps into my arms – mud and wet dog hair attaching to my once clean trousers and suit jacket. She wants her hug and she wants it now! As I bend down to her level, Dolce's paws wrap around my neck and she starts to lick my face.

Amore is next. She has pawed her way between Dolce and myself, inserting her body between, over, and under any arm that could and would pet her. Amore has pushed Dolce out of the way so she can get petted. I'm still bent over.

Not to be outdone, Tiamo has come from behind, pushing between the back of my legs, her head appearing between my crotch. She wants her head and ears scratched, and Tiamo always gets what she wants. She's our queen.

By now, my nylons are shredded, my purse dumped into a shallow puddle of leftover rain water, my leather briefcase now has a muddy paw print on the left side and my eyeglasses are a skewed from being bumped and jumped on by Dolce. I'm a filthy, dog-haired mess. The dogs don't care. Mom is home and they are glad to see me.

It takes me a good fifteen minutes before I'm able to settle our canine heathens down in order to swing and stagger a path into the house, dogs in tow.

Tiamo is still wanting her ears itched, is still between my legs. Dolce is jumping beside me, wanting back up in my arms. Amore on the other side of me wanting more petting between the ears. Somewhere, Malcolm has disappeared. Some welcome home!

I make it inside, the girls still excited. They missed me. Within another ten minutes they are sprawled on the couch, already asleep. Already tired out from my welcome home attack. I look for Malcolm.

Malcolm had barricaded himself in the den, armed with the newspaper and a glass full of shaved ice filled with his favored Coca-Cola.

Malcolm didn't surface for an appearance for five hours.

THE FLIRT

Tiamo was a flirt – a big flirt! She liked batting her big brown eyes, especially with males, big Bernese Mountain Dog males. She'd see a handsome male Berner and her Paris Hilton head-tilt along with her come-hither look would appear. Her tail a-swishing, her prance more pronounced, and a certain gleam in her eye would materialize each and every time a big studley, cutie-paw-tootie male dog was in the vicinity. Tiamo was shameless. Yep, you could definitely say Tiamo was a flirt!

The first time I noticed her flirting, Tiamo was around nine months old. I was walking her around the neighborhood loop where we live, when another Berner owner happened to drive by. He stopped to talk shop, as fellow Bernese Mountain Dog owners like to do.

He had his male Berner with him and let him out of the car to introduce the two. Shubert was a handsome 4-year-old male. He was a rehab dog for the elderly, fit with a deep chest, massive paws and weighing a hefty 125 lbs.; i.e., he was a poster child for Berner perfection. No doubt about it, he was one masculine and handsome dude. Because of his rehab training, Shubert was well behaved, especially around people.

Tiamo immediately took a shine to him. One look from Shubert and she fell in love. She puffed out her pre-adolescent chest, lifted up her tail and strutted over. She was in love.

When Shubert laid down in the shade of the car, Tiamo laid down as well, as close to Shubert as possible, rubbing shoulders, tail flicking, paws touching his, her head tilting. When Shubert crossed his front paws, Tiamo would mimic his actions and did the same. When Shubert lowered his head, Tiamo lowered hers. Puppy love was in bloom.

As we wrapped up our conversation, Shubert loaded up into the car, ready to go – Tiamo, not wanting to lose her new boyfriend, hopped right in the car behind him, scooting over to lean up against him. She'd found herself a real man and wasn't going to let him go. It took me a full ten minutes to con-slash-drag her out of the vehicle.

Never faithful for long, Tiamo moved on to greener pastures. Her next love affair was with Gus, a Bernese re-located from back east. Gus was the kind of guy that tightened the kink in her tail. A cougar worth her salt, Tiamo liked her men young and Gus was younger by 10 months.

His swagger down pat, his moves slick as silk, Gus was a ladies' man, a gigolo, a smooth operator and had all the canine ladies panting. Tiamo had met her match – she was one of many in a long line of lusting females but that didn't stop her. Gus was a dog that was handsome plus! Sparks ignited when the two were together, resulting in eight puppies, sixty plus days later.

Yes sirree, Gus fathered her beautiful children. And, then left her. A single mother, raising eight kids alone, you would think Tiamo would learn her lesson.

But nooooo, eleven months later, Tiamo was up to her old philandering ways.....

A couple of times a year, we try to bring the girls into the groomers' for a wash, cut and curl. We clip their bellies and their forearm feathers to keep the stickers and cockleburs to a minimum and it helps the dogs stay cool in the hot summer months.

It's not an easy process, bringing three big Bernese dogs to the groomers. Especially since they ALL dislike going there. War breaks out – dogs against humans.

Tiamo, particularly, did not like the process, protesting immediately upon entering the door to the groomers. Her front paws put on the brakes, stopping all forward movement into the establishment. She quickly put her back paws in full reverse, madly scrambling to dodge her fate. With her tail in fast fan mode and her body wiggling to get free, every toy and treat display in the front retail area was in the war zone. It's just a matter of timing when the displays come crashing down from a swipe of her tail or from a frantic escape move of her body.

Tiamo will ignore all commands to stop acting like a brat and to behave, seeking only to avoid her bath. She didn't so much mind the bath as she did the clippers. She hated the clippers. And she abhorred the colorful little bandana souvenir they tied around her neck at the end of the bath, trying to bite it off on the way home.

It got so bad, that we started bringing her in through the back door to minimize the damage to the store's displays in the front.

Until the day she saw Owen.

Owen was a local male Berner, proud, masculine, manly, he easily tipped the scales at 135 lbs. That boy was one handsome dog and he oooooooozed sex. He was a heartthrob. Movie star material.

Owen was already in the back wash rack when I arrived with Tiamo at the rear door, hoping upon hope she wouldn't put up too much of a fuss as we entered.

One sniff and the game was up. Tiamo knew full well she had been double-crossed. Duped into getting bathed and clipped, a full-on Tiamo tantrum erupted. She was not going to take a bath.

Nope, not gonna happen. Not today, not any day. No way, no how. The bathing battle was on.

Tiamo changed her delaying tactics and dropped to the tiled floor, rolling over on her back, four paws in the air, she was dead weight. Couldn't be picked up, dragged, moved or maneuvered. There were going to be no baths today. I was defeated and she knew it. Tiamo had won this bathing combat.

And then, out of the corner of her eye, she saw Owen. Oh boy, oh boy, oh boy! This was a new verse to the same old song.

Her ears twitched, her eyes glowed with that familiar glint, drool droplets trickled from her lips, her tail curled into a constricted ringlet. It only took one look from Owen for Tiamo to go gaga over him. Tiamo had a new love.

Miraculously, she spun upright, gave a little bitch shake, pulled her shoulders back, pushed her deep barreled chest out and pranced right up the ramp to her wash tub. An empty wash tub that happened to sit right next door to Owen's. With a flick of her tail, Tiamo had a new man. Owen didn't know what hit him. Owen was bowled over. Tiamo soon had Owen sharing his spaghetti. I stared at her in awe and amazement trying to figure out this new development.

Unapologetic for her earlier tantrum, Tiamo gave me the signal to leave, she had this handled. I quickly turned to leave. Exiting out the door, I peeked back at the two love-birds. Tiamo had jumped the tub's railing and was skinny-dipping with Owen. I kept walking. Thank gawd she's been spayed.

SAM

Malcolm and I don't have children – we have dogs. Use to be three, now two huge, wonderfully sweet, spoiled brats. Both of us were in our forties when we meet and married, well beyond the age to consider kids. But still young enough to fall into the pet trap.

Like most parents with real kids, Tiamo, our first Bernese Mountain Dog, was easy to raise and didn't give us any trouble. Much. We spent hours training her, socializing her, correcting her, loving her.

Santa Fe is a dog friendly town, permitting canines on leash most everywhere and we took her everywhere that allowed dogs. She was part of our family, we were part of her pack. There was never a time she wasn't with either Malcolm or I.

Tiamo would sit at our feet, under the table, while we sat outside eating lunch at the local cafes and bistros. She loved to watch the other patrons, always hoping there might be other dogs around. She was so well-behaved, little nippers would climb all over her and she loved the attention. She loved people and other animals, especially Thugs.

But most of all, she **LOVED** Sam.

Sam was our nephew and was loved like a son. In so many ways, he was the kid we never had.

One freezing cold January day, Sam arrived in Santa Fe. He arrived shirtless, in shorts and wearing flip-flops. He planned to stay for a short weekend visit. He was passing through New Mexico on his way to life.

I had never "truly" met this nephew of Malcolm's. He attended our wedding, but like most brides on the wedding day, I didn't remember much. As for Malcolm, it had been years since he had any true contact with him. Short emails and such, but no one-on-one, face-to-face conversations. In truth, neither one of us knew Sam very well, and me not at all. Neither one of us knew what to expect. I have no doubt Sam felt the same way.

Sam was 23 years, not even a quarter of a century old, and traveling through his life. While both Malcolm and I were fast approaching the half-dollar mark and getting ready to slide down the other side. Sam was just starting on his expedition, his life's trek. We were winding down from ours. We were poles apart on where we all were in our lives, in age, in experiences, and in goals. Somehow we managed to find common ground and meet in the middle.

My plan was to cook up a storm, for in my experience, food solved all dilemmas. Sam was in his early twenties, an age when all males ate a lot, extra servings and seconds, so double batches were required. I went to work in the kitchen.

Malcolm's plan was to show Sam around town, drive up through the mountains, expose Sam to the wonders of Santa Fe. Malcolm gassed up the SUV.

Sam's plan was to document life through his travels, videoing his journey, recording his thoughts. He had graduated from college and his young artist's soul was begging to be set free and loose in the wilds. His jump off was Santa Fe. He had tricked out his truck and camper into a cozy living area. He jimmy-rigged a camera mount on his bicycle to record his wanderings, pulled some money from his savings and had a full tank of gas and ideas. Ready. Set. Go.

He never left Santa Fe. One week later, after living in his truck at the Wal-Mart parking lot, Sam moved into our household, taking over the guest bedroom.

I had someone new to spoil, while Malcolm had someone new with which to impart wisdom and advice. Not having kids, we loved the fact he came diaper free and with manners. He was trained. We bonded quickly and the three of us became a family. We loved Sam - Sam loved us. Sam was special. Unique. We "adopted" him without any hesitation.

When Malcolm was turning fifty, I surprised him with a Bernese Mountain Dog puppy. Born on Thanksgiving Day, Tiamo joined our new family when she was eleven weeks old. We all instantly fell in love with her, especially Sam. Although, I think he originally saw her as a chick magnet with four legs and fur. I mean, seriously, what female under 80 and not blind, would not fall in love with a Bernese puppy! For that matter, Sam was a hottie. What female under 30 and/or blind would not fall for a tall handsome Texan.

Sam took part in Tiamo's training. He assisted in walking her, grooming her and teaching her to sit, along with other commands. Sam would volunteer to bring Tiamo to the vet when she needed her booster shots. He took care of Tiamo when we went away for travel and trips. Sam was Tiamo's third caregiver. The two of them were inseparable.

When Sam later moved into town, I think he missed Tiamo more than he missed us. I know Tiamo missed him something fierce. She would go absolutely nuts when Sam came to visit and wouldn't leave his side. Malcolm and I were ignored. For Tiamo, Sam was it.

Tiamo would have this goofy grin on her face when Sam showed up. Her eyes would light up and she would prance around, showing off for Sam. Sam always brought her a treat. Something special just for her. It got so every time Sam came, she would immediately reach for his pant's pocket, nosing her muzzle, sniffing for her treat. Sam never failed to disappoint her.

Tiamo was the happiest when the three of us were together. Sam, Malcolm and I. Plus Tiamo. She would grab her toy of the week, gnawing on it while laying at our feet, listening to our voices as we caught up on our lives. Her family together, Tiamo was happy and content.

Sam loved the outdoors. Even on the coldest of days, he and Malcolm would sit outside, watching the sun disappear behind the horizon, enjoying a glass of wine, a bottle of beer, discussing life. They would pull up two old wooden rocking chairs to the edge of the portal, facing west, and observe the sky's colors as they faded from brilliant blue to fiery orange to pitch black. Tiamo at their feet. They would still be talking as the stars turned on their lights, twinkling from above. Tiamo was content to be with her "boys", Sam and Malcolm.

Some nights, Malcolm and Sam would light a small fire in the clay Chiminea for warmth. Other times, they would gently rock their chairs to the cadence of their conversation, low murmurs that would tease Tiamo into a soft sleep at their feet. During the summer months, Sam and Malcolm would take Tiamo for midnight walks after it had cooled down from the day's heat. Tiamo happily trotting along besides the two of them. Plainly said, Tiamo LOVED Sam.

When Sam was 27, he passed away. The first year, after Sam's death, was the hardest. Malcolm and I had to re-adjust our family back down to two with a dog. Along with Tiamo, we had to re-adjust to never seeing Sam again. We all mourned. We all missed Sam. Like barbed wire twisted around our hearts, we felt every razor-sharp prong squeezing into our grief and sorrow. Our hearts were bleeding, bruised and beat up. Tiamo's was as well.

The following spring after Sam's death, I started a memorial garden. West of our covered portal, in full view of the day's end, I planted flowery shrubs, bushes and flowers in every color to remind us of the sun winking good night. Fiery reds and oranges, brilliant blue hues, twinkling whites and luminous purples. Cheerful yellows and soft pinks. Bright colors to reflect life's wonder. Colorful shades of nature reminiscent of watching the sun disappear behind the Sandias as all of us conversed. A salute to our loved ones. A nod to Sam. We missed our Sam, but are so thankful he joined our life for what little time we had with him.

We have since laid flagstone, moved the clay Chiminea pot to the middle of the stonework and added more wooden rocking chairs. Birdhouses and yard art are scattered around to commemorate the joy of life. Sam's life. Bright colors surround the garden, flowers edging the stone's perimeter. Pinon, pine trees and junipers providing the shade and adding a wind break. It has become a happy place. It is a continual work in progress.

Tiamo was half way through her sixth year when Malcolm and I had to put her down. Cancer. Heart-wrenching. Sad. Deep. We had two weeks to prepare for the finality of losing her. We had been through the grief of losing Sam. Now we were going to go through the heartache and anguish of losing another beloved child.

There was no question that we would bury Tiamo at home in our Memorial Garden. A place where Tiamo would sit at Sam's feet as Malcolm and Sam watched the sun set. Malcolm had chosen an area in the garden where Tiamo loved to lay while Sam and Malcolm chatted, solving the world's problems. Under a big juniper tree, he started to dig her burial plot.

As Malcolm prepared Tiamo's final resting spot, Tiamo laid by the deepening hole and watched, silently giving us her acceptance of what was to come. She was ready. We were not.

We didn't want to let her go. Memories of her as a puppy, remembrances of Sam "borrowing" Tiamo to assist him in picking up long-legged co-eds, recollections of Tiamo sitting at our feet while sitting on the portal, flooded our hearts. Our beautiful

Tiamo was in pain. No more walks on the green belt, no more belly rubs at night, no more trips in the car. We knew it wouldn't be long.

Our veterinarian had told us we would know when to bring her in. "When it's time to stop the suffering, you'll know," she said, her eyes filled with sympathy.

Malcolm and I felt like we were playing at being God, making the decision about when to end Tiamo's life, when to "bring her in." "When it was time" turned into "then it was time" way too soon. With tears in our eyes and a heavy, burdened heart, we put Tiamo down. Again, Malcolm and I deeply grieved.

When we bring pets into our lives, we come to the understanding that, most likely we will outlive them by many years. Most likely there will be many other pets in between. We had already put Thugs down, our aging cat of nearly twenty-two years. And our Hollywood, movie star cats, John Wayne and Marilyn Monroe. You'll read more about them in the next chapter. Malcolm and I accepted that. Hate it, but know it, and know this is life. Damn it hurts.

We buried Tiamo in her favorite spot, shaded by junipers and surrounded by color, facing west to watch the sun set. She is close to Thugs, her BFF for years. She is deeply missed.

I would like to believe Sam and Tiamo are high in the sky, in their happy place together. Tiamo has her "Sam" to play with, sniffing out an endless supply of treats from his pockets, prancing around in a field of soft green clover. Sam has Tiamo, keeping him company while he enjoys the outdoors.

We miss our kids.

the mutt manuscripts

APPLE SNATCHING

Every year, Malcolm, my husband, ever the rural gardener (NOT!), decides to plant fruit trees. Cherries, peaches, apricots, apples, you name it. And every year, he has high hopes of a bumper crop.

Unfortunately, we live in an area where the wind blows right about the time the blossoms are popping on the tree, blowing away any glimmer and all chances of fruit off the branches. Our March winds show up in early February and usually last through June or July. There is not a snow-ball's chance in hell a future fruit blossom can handle the abuse from our strong winds that sneeze across the land.

Plus, we live at an elevation of 7,000 feet where it can easily snow into the month of May, freezing the promise of juicy sweetness. If the wind and the freeze don't destroy any chance of apples, by late August, the coyotes come through and feed off of the trees. They leave a barren fruit line at the four foot and below mark. The coyotes just can't reach any higher.

Needless to say, at best, we might be able to pick a dozen or so of token apples, just enough to bake a pie – a small pie that we can claim the apples grew in our garden.

One year, we were able to pick and gather two huge baskets of apples. I left them on our high kitchen counter to use at a later date. I assured myself there was no way the dogs could get to the apples. The counter was over five feet tall. However, each day when I came home from work, I noticed the pile of apples was becoming significantly smaller. Naturally, I assumed my husband was pigging out on apples. Of course, Malcolm naturally presumed I was taking apples into work, sharing the homegrown apples with my co-workers.

To our surprise, we learned differently....

To keep the mouse population down, we have cats. Since cats are on the bottom of the food chain, unfortunately, we don't always have them for long. There was a time when we had two young kittens. A brother and sister duo, they were gorgeous felines. We called them our movie star cats – John Wayne and Marilyn Monroe.

The Duke, a large male with handsome coloring, had a swagger and a stance just like John Wayne. He could belly up to the bar and be in control. Look across the room and pick out the bad guys, take a swig and charge into the fray. That was our Duke.

Now Marilyn, she was dainty as well as she was beautiful. Perfect white paws, a white ruffled collar, fluffy calico fur, absolutely stunning. She would sashay her hips, swinging her fluffy tail like seaweed in a gentle tide. She could, and did, give all of us little peons a come whither look. With a pout on her lips and a flick of her tail, she commanded attention. We were at her beck and call. That was our Marilyn.

Tiamo, Amore and Dolce pretty much got along with our Hollywood felines. Dolce kept her distance in the beginning, not wanting her nose to feel the sharp end of a claw, and Tiamo tolerated the two, but all-in-all, the cats and the dogs were one big happy family.

We soon learned they were more than just a one big happy family. Duke and Marilyn had joined forces with our three Berners. Together, our sweet little kitties and our three big dogs were devouring the apples.

Waiting until we were out of the house, Duke and Marilyn would jump up onto the tall counter where the large baskets of apples sat. They understood if we were home, they would not be allowed on the counter. A huge water spritzer stayed close by, ready to spray misbehaving cats should they attempt to jump to the counter.

It's true when they say "when the cats away, the mouse will play." Our animal kingdom simply waited until we were gone, away from the house, before they began there misbehaving antics.

The shinny red apples must have looked like nirvana to our cats. Toys. Big and bright. A beacon of red. Just the right size to play with. Just round enough to knock around, to see where it rolls. How could any cat, or dog for that matter, resist. Duke's big paws reached in the basket to bat an apple out to the counter, where Marilyn waited her turn. It was inevitable an apple would tumble to the floor, where three canines were eagerly waiting. In one chomp, the apple would disappear down the throat of a dog.

John Wayne and Marilyn grew bolder. Way too confident, they over played their hand, letting greed take over – one day, they forgot we were still at home. The little brats! They were all in cahoots together! Tag teaming.

We watched from the hallway, spying on all of them, as the cats batted the apples down to the dogs. In less than a week, the apples were gone. Disappeared.

Watching the antics of three dogs madly scrambling to catch the apple before the other two could was hilarious! Watching Marilyn and John Wayne toy with the dogs, knowing they were in control, was more so. You could see the cats thinking; "silly dogs, going crazy over these shiny red balls." Watching the five of them playing together was totally worth losing two baskets of apples.

The next year our apple tree was loaded with fruit. I mean loaded. To the max. It was a bumper year for apples in Santa Fe.

Anybody with an apple tree in their back yard was giving bags of fruit away to their neighbors and friends. Having survived the wind and any possible freeze, the branches were bowing to the ground with the heavy weight of its produce. Only now it wasn't the coyotes we needed to worry about – it was Dolce! The little stinker had learned a new trick.

Hanging low enough for Dolce to reach, she couldn't resist the forbidden fruit. Tempting, taunting, Dolce couldn't withstand the sweet enticement. Once out the back door, Dolce would high tail it down to the apple tree, burrowing into the apple rich branches, she would sniff for the perfect fruit, grab the apple in her muzzle, gobble it down and go back for more.

She loves the tug and the snap of the fruit as she is pulling it off the branch. She knows at that exact moment the apple is hers!

When the branch springs back from her wrench, when the water droplets on the leaves from the recent rains splash onto her face, when the resistance of ownership transfers from the tree to her muzzle, she knows she is the victor. And, let me tell 'ya, she is one happy camper! Shiny bright eyes, a mouth full of apple and believe it or not, a grin of pure happiness.

It didn't take long for Amore to join the apple caper exploitation. Only Amore didn't quite understand the proper apple picking procedures. She only knew Dolce was eating apples and she wasn't. I'm not sure if she just doesn't like tunneling her head into the dense thicket of leaves and branches, searching for the perfect fruit, or if she is just dog gone lazy. But to this day, Amore has yet to pull an apple from the tree.

However she is smart enough to patiently wait for Dolce to build her silo of apples and then steal 'em straight from Dolce's pile.

Dolce would harvest five or six shinny red orbs and then lay down underneath the tree in the cool shade to snack. While Dolce's mouth was full, Amore would approach, snatching a treat from Dolce's mound, then running away to a safe spot to eat it. Dolce seemed to be okay doing all the work. I think her favorite part of the adventure was pulling the apples off the tree.

That year, even with Dolce assisting in the picking, we had so many apples, we ran out of storage space. Our extra refrigerator in the garage was loaded to capacity with apples. Every bucket, basket and bin was filled to the brim with apples. We ended up placing several baskets outside, under our back portal until we could give the tasty fruit away or process them. The nights were starting to drop in temperature, the days were cooler after the hot summer. The apples would be at a safe enough temperature.

Dolce still sprinted down to the tree when let out the back door, checking for any left over fruit, only now the tree was picked clean. The tempting fruit had all but disappeared. She would poke her head around, sniffing for her treats. The leaves had turned brown, floating to the ground as mother nature was preparing for hibernation, before Dolce acknowledged there wasn't any more fruit to be picked. Yet she still poked her nose in the branches on the tree, still sniffing for one more delectable delicacy. Investigating for one last apple. One more delicious treat. Nil, none, nada. Dolce had eaten all the apples hanging low enough for her to reach. Her disappointment was keen.

It was about a month later that we took Dolce and Amore to the vet for their annual check up. Both Dolce and Amore needed their rabies booster and it was time for some teeth cleaning.

Taking the girls to the vet is always a major project. They both associate the vet's clinic with pain and unpleasantness, needles and shots, procedures and surgeries. Once we make the turn into the parking lot, Dolce and Amore are filled with dread. Their anxiousness is evident. The front paw brakes are set and locked. It's a contest of wills and muscle to get them inside the doors. Doable, but not easily.

Our vet clinic is a brand new, state-of-the-art facility. Built and designed especially for the ease and comfort of the animals and pets that are brought in. Felines have a special room to avoid dog panic. Canines have a spacious waiting area to avoid an alpha dog spat. Waiting our turn, I had Dolce on my lap, all 100 pounds, shaking and shivering with trepidation.

The vet tech calls our name and ushered us over to the built-in floor scale. Weigh-in time.

"Umm, looks like Dolce has gained a bit of weight since we last saw her," the tech commented as she scanned Dolce's chart.

"Have you been feeding her differently?" she asked benignly.

"That's odd, we've fed her the same amount for the last two years....?" we were puzzled over her increase in poundage.

"Check Amore's weight. See if she has expanded?" we requested. Amore's weight had stayed the same, no gain. Malcolm and I looked at each other. Was Dolce eating Amore's food? Did we need to separate their feed bowls? It's always a pain in the ass to have to measure out different amounts of dog food at feeding time. Trying to keep it straight, which dog gets what amount can be confusing. It was a bigger pain to separate them. The two girls had grown up eating side-by-side.

Dolce had gained a good ten plus pounds. She went from a svelte 85 lbs. to a hefty 97. Our vet likes to see the girls weigh between 85 to 88 lbs. On average, Bernese Mountain Dog females will weigh between 85 to 100 lbs. depending on their height. Berner males average 100 to 125 lbs. Tiamo, their mother, tended to be on the hefty side, causing periodic concern when she tipped the scales. We always tried to keep their weight constant.

We didn't get it. We were very conscious of their weight. We walked Dolce and Amore daily, anywhere from two to four miles with some fairly steep inclines thrown in for a good cardio workout. We measured their food. Spent extra change on a special brand that does not have filler such as corn or wheat in the product. What the hell was going on? We were puzzled.

Okay. I confess. Occasionally, I would buy them pig ears when I'm at the feed store, and sometimes a jerky treat, but nothing out of the ordinary. Malcolm and I agreed, no more special treats, no more indulgences. Dolce was on a diet. Die with a T. A capital T. Come hell or high water, our canine piglet was going to slim down to a healthier size.

We were into November, daylight savings had turned off the late lights, the days too chilly to spend much time on the back portal. It was time to winterize our summer outdoor room. It was time to put away our pillows and chair pads, store our wicker furniture in the garage. Malcolm was stacking chairs, I was stuffing pillows into storage bins when I heard laughter and chuckles coming from Malcolm, loud chortles.

I turn to look over at Malcolm, checking to see what was so funny. Malcolm is holding up the huge, I mean huge, apple basket. Empty. The apples gone. Dolce had eaten all the stored apples. All of'em!

"That's why she gained the weight! She probably was eating ten to twelve apples a day!" he hooted. Doing the math in my head, Malcolm was right. I calculated the number of days we had stored the apples on the portal to the approximate number of apples in the basket. Mystery solved.

When Dolce couldn't find any apples on the tree, she would run back up to the portal where the baskets were stored to seize another juicy prize. Dolce could easily wolf down three to four apples while our backs were turned.   And then go back for seconds.

We knew Dolce liked to grab an apple. We didn't realize she was practically devouring them when our backs were turned.

Dolce would wait until we were looking away, then double-back to the portal to grab an apple. Chomping quickly before we noticed. Scarfing them down as fast as she could before we saw.

She is sneaky, our Dolce. She can chomp and swallow in a nano-second. Two seconds and it's disappeared, down the hatch and into the gully.

Our apple-snatching thief was caught.

TAHMATAHS

Malcolm is a Georgia boy, born and raised. One thing this Georgia boy loves is Tah-mat-ahs! Those of us that hail from the West Coast call them tomatoes.

In the South, especially in Georgia, homegrown "tahmatahs" are a source of delight. Malc is always going on about their southern tahmatahs.

"Tahmatahs," he'd say, drawing out the syllables. According to Malcolm, only Yankees up North or myself from California, pronounce it as tomato.

Vine ripened, big, red, flavorful tahmatahs. And, he complains about how you just can't find a good home-grown, sun-ripened tahmatah in "this God Forsaken desert."

Out in the rural areas of Georgia, where you'll find an abundance of back yard produce, growing a good tahmatah is a like winning the community best award. Like baking the best apple pie at the county fair. It's a reputation kind of thing. Locals are known for their tahmatahs. Just like Aunt Betty Sue is known for her pimento cheese spread, the local farmers are known for their produce, good or bad.

Unfortunately, Northern New Mexico's isn't known for its tomatoes. Chilies yes, tomatoes no. Our growing season starts late and ends early. It's hard to grow a tasty tomato in such a short growing time. It's equally hard to be hailed as the "he grows the best tomatoes" neighbor or the "this stand has the best tomatoes" vendor.

Farmers at our world famous Santa Fe Farmers Market will let you sample before you buy, tempting the buyer through their taste buds. They try hard to prove their produce is better tasting, better looking, just all round better. Let me tell ya', it's good, it's even great, but it ain't Georgia good. That Georgia red clay does something to a tahmatah.

Homegrown tahmatahs are always a treat around our house and always graciously accepted if offered some to take home. Malcolm will never turn down a tahmatah. They are a coveted possession. Add a little salt and pepper, perhaps some olive oil, and my Georgia boy is in heaven.

It just so happened, I had been given some homegrown tomatoes while visiting at a friend's house. Five nice sized tomatoes. Five homegrown tomatoes. Five "he grows great tomatoes" from the neighbor tomatoes.

Picked at just the right time, they were firm, not soft or mushy. They were on the larger size as well, not small, nor even medium sized. Crinkly valleys at the top where the prickly green stem was once attached, they were slightly misshaped with a deep purplish red hue to their skin. Still warm from the sun, these weren't your toss in the salad kind of tomatoes. These were perfect, eat by themselves kinds of tahmatahs.

Paper bagged, I set the produce on the dashboard over by the passenger side, away from twelve huge dog paws that have little to no regard for anything placed within paw range, as I drove towards home. I had brought the dogs with me as I journeyed over to our friend's place.

"Hey, honey, guess what I have for ya?" I taunted him on the cell phone as I drove home, knowing full well he would have no idea of the treat I was bringing to him. After playing the "what game." I informed him I was bringing him home some home grown tahmatahs.

"Hot damn!" Malc was excited! It was at the end of our growing season and good tomatoes were getting scarce. I could picture Malcolm salivating over his treat. I knew he was already pulling out the olive oil and seasonings from the cupboard. Malcolm would be drooling as he was getting prepared for his tahmatahs!

As I pulled up to the driveway, I stopped the car at the top of our graveled road and hopped out to get the mail. I had all three dogs with me and left them in the car. As our mailbox is directly across the dirt road from our driveway, I put the car in park, set the brake and quickly jumped out to retrieve our mail. We do this all the time as it only takes a few seconds before we then roll the car down the slight descent into the garage.

But a few seconds was all the girls needed. I doubt I had been out of the car for more than three seconds total, when they decided to poke their noses into mischief. I'm not sure who was first to grab the bag off the dash, but all three where chowing down on four of the five just picked off the vine Tahmatahs by the time I got back to the car with a handful of junk mail and flyers. Tomato juice and seeds spewed all over the back seat. There were happy grins on all three dogs. If we learned anything that day, we learned the dogs will eat anything – even tomatoes!

They left us one precious juicy red tomato. It was obvious Malcolm and I were going to have to share. Not a good scenario when both of us are the youngest of many siblings. When it comes to food, neither one of us does the "share" thing very well. Though I have to admit, Malcolm is better at it than I am. He seems resigned to me stealing a French Fry or two off his plate. Me? I have a fork in hand, tines pointed south, ready to stab the offensive hand trying to steal from my plate. I know of only one word to defend my plate. One-syllable. MINE!

Coming from a household that used the adage, "You cut, I pick" to stop fights over who got the biggest piece of pie, I knew this wasn't good. Malcolm is from the south where homegrown tahmatahs are as sacred as Sunday After Church Fried Chicken. I love him dearly, so I was weighing the mental scales of how much vs. the lone tomato. Do I share? Do I keep? Do I give? Just how much did I love him?

As I prepared dinner, I looked at the surviving tahmatah, checking out the misshapen size with its deep crevasses and divots. I had the good angel sitting on my left shoulder, encouraging me to give the whole tomato to Malcolm. I had the devilish imp on the other side, promoting "keep the tomato" for yourself, he'll never know. I also had three not-so-innocent canine faces staring up at me beseechingly for another chance at the last tomato. No one was going to win.

Problem was, Malcolm would know. He knew I was bringing home a bag full of tahmatahs. I just might be able to fool Malcolm into picking the "short-end of the stick" half of the tomato, but there was no way I could fool him out of nothing.

I knew just how much he loves his tahmatahs. Predictably, I gave Malcolm the whole thing and he has since showered me with diamonds and gold. It was a great trade!

SNOOZE BUTTON

A cold wet nose is thrust upon my sweet early morning dreams. I raised my bed-head to look at the bedroom alarm clock on the nightstand and tried to focus on the blue digital numbers.

Crap! It's only 4:05 a.m. There is still forty-five minutes before the alarm sounds off. I try to ignore the persistent nose nudging under my elbow, desperately wanting and needing my forty-five minutes more of additional shut-eye. I try to go back to sleep. Keeping my eyes closed, I feel another nose nudge, this time on my hand that is dangling over the edge of the bed outside of the covers.

!UGH!

Dog slobber. All over my hand. Uck! I open my sleep crusted eyes into slits, cracked ajar just enough to double-check the time. I don't want Dolce or Amore to see my eyes open. Dolce and Amore, with their twin cold noses, are within centimeters of my face, eyeing me intently. Hopeful, they waiting with baited breath to see if I'll get up.

Two sets of eyes, shining brightly, eagerly waiting for me to rise and start the day. Once I'm up, they know breakfast is just around the corner. That's what they really want. Food!

My eyes rise once again to the alarm clock. 4:10 a.m. – forty minutes left. It's only been five minutes. I close my eyes and pretend I'm asleep. No such luck.

!WHACK!

A sand encrusted paw hits the edge of the bed, just missing my nose. I am assaulted with dog-paw odor.

"Off"! I whisper, not wanting to wake up Malcolm. Amore doesn't listen to my command, nor does she care. Her only concern is wanting mom up and at 'em. That and her breakfast.

Whack! Another paw joins the first. More sand, more paw odors. I look up from my soft pillow, Amore is peering down on me with her happy dog face and her happy dog drool dripping onto my cheek and neck. Drip. Drip. It's pure water torture. Giving me her big lop-sided dog grin as she realizes I am watching her.

!UCK!

I go to wipe off the wet dog drool drops and smear wet sand all over me.

UGH! 4:20 a.m. I still have 30 minutes more. A half-hour nap is my only hope. I pray to the early morning dog gods to let me have my thirty minutes. Please. Just thirty more. Puleeze.

Amore licks my face, a more persistent dog you'll never see. She. Wants. Me. Up. NOW! I roll over, implementing the "if I can't see you, you can't see me" rule, feeling the rough sand throughout the sheets. It's not gonna happen, Amore wants me up.

!ICK!

Amore's determination runs deep as she paws the bed covers, pulling my warm blankets inch by coveted inch off the bed into a massive soft heap on the floor. The dog gods didn't come through.

4:37 a.m. I am now freezing, dog slobbered, sand-covered and wide-awake. Malcolm is softly snoring, oblivious to my early morning canine wake-up call.

Just then, Dolce leaps up on the bed, clears a sleeping Malcolm, and lands on me.

!PHOOF!

The oxygen is squished out of my lungs. I gasp for breath, simultaneously pushing Dolce off me. I manage to turn her around, only to have her victorious wagging tail in my face. The breeze from her tail wagging measuring the equivalent of gale-forced winds of a Category Five Hurricane.

UGH! Visions of sleeping extra minutes vanished along with all the air from my lungs. 4:43 a.m.

Not to be out done, Amore jumps onto the mattress, her paws digging into Malcolm's legs for balance.

"W.T.F.?"

Malcolm is rudely awakened. 4:45 a.m. I have five minutes till "Wake-Up with Wally" blasts out the top ten hits on FM 107.9. I shut off the alarm with Wally and crawl out of bed, crawl being the optimal word. The dogs are ecstatic they have some early morning company, which means breakfast will soon be coming. Malcolm is grumpy from being woken up. I was a snooze button away from being sane.

We've learned there is no snooze button for dogs who want their breakfast!

LEFT OVERS

L eft-overs. We all look forward to the Friday after Thanksgiving – the day that produces the holy mother-lode of all leftovers!

Turkey sandwiches, turkey enchiladas, turkey soup. And then there is sweet potato pancakes, potato balls and a lot gravy with a little mashed potatoes. Cold stuffing, Cornbread stuffing, and just being stuffed. Yep, Friday after Thanksgiving is the King of leftovers!

Sneaking into the kitchen late at night to nab the last slice of pumpkin pie, hiding the treats and cookies from Malcolm, standing over the kitchen sink feasting on day-old dinner scraps rather than wash another dirty plate. Lets face it! We've all done it. There is no proper etiquette when eating leftovers. It's a first come, first serve free-for-all. You snooze, you lose.

Each year, we swear on our full, bursting at the seams, bellies, that the next year we aren't going to eat so much or overindulge our drinks. Each year, we do anyway. Each year, we swear we are going to cut back on the menu, preparing less, and each year we add another "must-try" recipe that becomes a staple for the next Thanksgiving's table.

Each year, we try to give away the left-overs to our friends and guests as they are leaving for home and each year we end up with even more left-over filled Tupperware freshly burped in the fridge.

Tiamo, Dolce and Amore love the idea of leftovers. As puppies, Dolce and Amore loved the leftover pumpkin scraped out of the can used in the pie. Baking day will find them at the edge of the kitchen boundaries, hoping for some tasty morsel to land on the floor. And, Tiamo, well she just loves food.

They know the rule, if it falls on the floor, it's theirs! (loaded with fiber, pumpkin is actually good for little puppy tummies and their digestion). When the chef is in the kitchen prepping for the Thanksgiving dinner, these three mutts pray to the high canine heavens for dropped cheese crumbs, fallen turkey scraps and abandoned potato peels. Green beans, broccoli, even a brussel sprout. Anything.

They wish for an apple slice to fall, carrot chunks to plummet and diced celery to plunge off the chopping block and into their waiting jaws. It has become a contest between all of them, which one can snatch the dropped treasure first. Who can reach the fallen treat before the others. Whose nose has a quicker sniffer, catching the faint scent of some special delight.

My favorite leftover is pecan pie. Warm from the oven or cold for breakfast, pecan pie is my preferred holiday leftover dessert. It's my perfect midnight snack. A little whipped topping, a dab of ice cream (if there is any left) and a sliver of pecan pastry. Yummmm!

I've learned the hard way to hide the pie from Malc and the dogs.

GOOFY GIRL

Our Amore is a goof ball! A total klutz. A true dog ditz. A ham for the camera. A jester for the court. She is all of the above and then some.

There are times Malcolm and I think Amore hit her head on the sideboard of the whelping pen as she was dropped into being. The things she unwittingly does amazes us.

She has fallen off the couch more times than not, thunking to the floor as she was stretching while on her back. Surprise lights up her eyes as she tries to pretend that was her intention to begin with. She has chased after phantom bunnies and the shadows of high soaring hawks only to run into low-hanging juniper branches. She would rather have her throat scratched than her belly rubbed and would rather run than walk, even if it is just to move from one favorite spot to another, five short feet over.

If you say "sit," she hears "shit" and will begin a triple-axel spin to find the perfect spot. Give Amore the signal to "go to her pillow" and it's a sure bet it will be your down-pillow that she lies on.

She has no idea how to cuddle, coo or be calm. Wild-eyed, Amore will stare at you, and stare at you, and stare at you, never blinking, not moving, just stare at you. Intently. Don't try to out stare her – you won't win.

One of Amore's favorite antics is waking us up on weekends. The first attempt is a strong paw to your most extended limb poking out of the covers. The next try is a wet and cold nose nudge, usually on your neck, many times on your mouth.

The final act is a jump on the bed, normally with your sleeping body softening the landing as her front paws hit your stomach. At this point, Amore will typically sit on you, and the bed covers, trapping you underneath her. I don't mean sitting on one of your legs, or leaning up against your side. I mean a take-your-weight-off-your-paws-and-park-yourself down kind of stay awhile sit. Hundred pounds of canine on top of you.

By now you might be awake, but you ain't going anywhere til she decides to let up. It's best to get up at the first pawing. You can't help but chuckle to yourself as you spit dog hair off your lips while pushing her off you. Our goofy girl wants to share the early morning with you. Her love of life is amazing.

Amore's latest gimmick is scouting for lizards. She'll stand at attention, staring for hours waiting for a lizard to crawl up our stuccoed portal half-wall. Upon sighting a scaly blue-tail, she'll run to us, barking for us to come and see her find.

Occasionally, Amore will actually catch a lizard, bringing the four-legged "thing" into the house so she can play "search and seizure" with the now let-loose and tail-less reptile. Not that I particularly want a loose lizard in the house, but at least Gordita, our fatty catty, will catch the free-range lizard once Amore starts to fatigue from the game.

Goofy? Yes! Silly? Absolutely! Hyper? Undoubtedly! But our goofy girl is one of the happiest dogs I have ever seen. We are the lucky ones to have her adventures in our lives.

HELL BENT FOR LEATHER!

Amore loves to run. She runs just for the hell of it, just for the fun. She starts her day at full throttle, running through the hours from dawn to dusk. Why walk when you can run, has been her M.O. from the day she was born.

We're not talking about a slow trot or a little dog jog to catch up to us on the trail. We're talking the "hell bent for leather" kind of running. Full speed. Fast. Putting the brakes on only when there is a human knee one-eighth of an inch in front of her nose. The painful part of her running is that knee is always attached to Malcolm or myself. There are no half measures with Amore.

When Amore sees us putting on our hiking boots, she knows it is walk-time. She is beside herself with excitement, knowing she'll get to run, run, run. To her heart's content. Her tail starts to wag, her body starts to shake and wiggle. Barking full of excitement comes next, then she'll race back and forth, throughout the house, sprinting from the front door to back door, trying to anticipate which exit we'll take. It's walk time!

With a given cue, Amore and Dolce can be out the gate and into the car in less than three seconds flat. They are ready for their walk. They can cut the load-up time in half if the tailgate on the SUV is already turned down and the truck is backed up to the gate. There is no dilly-dallying around. Their walks, also known as runs, are serious business.

We like to take the girls out to the Galisteo Basin Preserve for their daily walk. There are some great hiking trails and the two love to chase jackrabbits and cottontails. The GBP is only a few miles down the road, it's quiet, not a lot of people know about the

Preserve (as of yet) and we're able to let them run off leash without worrying.

Amore is our scout when on the trail. She'll dart ahead of us, looking for movement of any kind. Birds, lizards, horny-toads, she is off like a shot when her attention is grabbed. She gets about fifty yards ahead, looking back at us, confirming we're still a-coming, still in sight, then scamper after her next quarry, running the whole time. Hell bent for leather!

A couple years ago, we started training them to return to us at the shrill of a whistle. We would reward them with a treat when they hustled back to us, making them sit before they received their peanut butter flavored incentive. It worked like a charm.

As their training progressed, as they continued to get better at returning, we would wait until Amore and Dolce were just out-of-sight, behind a juniper or over a rise in the terrain, then blow the whistle, testing them for their quick responses. Hell bent, they would race back to us, eager for the special reward for returning at the whistle.

For once, Amore picked up on the game quickly – knowing there was a treat to be had. She would race ahead, then run full speed back, many times without being called, sitting at our feet waiting for her treat. If we didn't give her the goods, she would stand in front of us, blocking us from moving forward, not letting us pass. She had been good, doing what she was taught, she was determined to get her nibble, so what if we didn't blow the shrill whistle.

One time, just as we were starting out on our hike, Amore sped past us up the path. looped around a Pinon tree that was only ten yards ahead and came back in a hurry. She sat down and gave us that look that said, "see-how-good-I-am-now-give-me-my-treat!"

Now Dolce is another story. She is smarter and wiser. She usually trots behind us in our wake, letting Amore get a ways up the trail. When we blow the whistle, she scoots in front of us, sitting on her haunches, already in place, waiting for the promised treat. Dolce has figured out she has a 80% chance she just might get an extra treat thrown to her before Amore arrives back. Smart dog that she is, she usually does get that extra treat!

Dolce is our sniffer. She takes after her mother, Tiamo, in this regard. While Amore has raced ahead, Dolce likes to lollygag her way throughout our treks, pausing regularly to check out the neighborhood. She'll stop to smell who's been by, sniff every low hanging branch and leaf, examining what wildlife has passed, leaving her scent on every weed and bush. Malcolm likes to joke she is reading the local paper, catching up on the local news.

Dolce is especially crafty when it comes to eating something she's not supposed to while on trail. She'll hang back behind us, just far enough that she's able to nab a horse apple before you can call her on it. She knows she is not to eat leftover trail dung. Horse crap on a dog's breath is NOT pleasant!

Malcolm and I pay the price on those weather-ridden days the girls don't get their walk. We try hard not to miss a day of exercising them. Two dogs, full of energy, cooped up in a house is not a good scenario. Shoes go missing, toilet paper gets shredded, and area rugs become re-arranged. Hell bent for leather indoors doesn't work with me.

Then the sumo wrestling match starts – body slamming and tail chasing is not an indoor sport. Leapfrog is next on the playlist. The entertainment and competition is fierce. Dolce has the lead in jumping. Amore wins hands down on speed. They are two for two for most creative crashes.

Like those parents who tote their children to sports practice at 5:00 a.m. in the morning, we drive our "kids" to the Basin for their walk. In the snow, cold and wind, (I don't do rain) we bring the girls to their special spot of nature and let 'em run and sniff to their heart's content. Hell bent for leather.

The happiness in their eyes is worth it.

THE BABY-SITTER

It starts with a phone call – a call where immediately you know something is wrong, awfully wrong. Every warning bell in your brain goes off. Your internal antenna goes on full alert, frantically searching for a false signal of normalcy to beat back the dreadful feeling that something bad has happened. The tone of the voice on the other end is somber. It's slow and deep, contrasting with your own erratic heartbeat and pulse.

Instinctively, you take a deep breath, bracing yourself for what's to come....

I'm out-of-town, three states over at a National Conference for my work, sitting in the middle of a meeting. My cell phone is silenced – if I hadn't of looked down at the exact moment when the screen lit up as the call came through, I would have missed the call all together. It's Malcolm.

My first thought is to call him back when my meeting is over in another 30 minutes. He knew I would be in back-to-back sessions all day long and I would call him later that evening when I got back to my hotel room.

My next thought brings a tightening of the stomach muscles. Malcolm knows I've turned the ringer off and am out-of-pocket for the day. Why would he call?

My gut tenses as I quickly gather my belongings and step outside the conference room to answer the call.

"Can you talk?" breaks the silence as I answer the call. Just his tone alone immediately tells me there is a problem. My eyes search for a quiet corner where I can't be overheard. Fortunately I find a private area with a sitting bench, across the wide conference hall. I sit down, turning my back to the conference activity behind me.

"I'm at the vet's," Malcolm somberly informs me, filling the long distanced silence across the phone lines. I hear the anxiety in his voice.

At once I'm both relieved Malcolm is okay and worried about which one of the dogs has been brought into our vet clinic. On a Saturday. Late in the afternoon. It had to be serious if it couldn't wait until Monday. My stomach tightens into a twisted knot.

"Who? Why? What? How?" The questions rapidly spewed out like the staccato of high heels on a hardwood floor.

"Amore. She swallowed a bone. It's lodged at the base of her esophagus, just above her stomach. They can't get it to move into her stomach, it's too far down her throat. It's stuck." Malcolm's somber tone added to my anxiety.

Of all the dogs, Amore is the one who has seen the vet's office the most. Our energetic girl, our runner, was once again brought to her knees. I took a deep breath and braced myself for whole story.

There was a long drawn out pause before Malcolm added, "Honey, it doesn't look good." Malcolm's voice was terse, his worry and tension evident as he broke the news to me. He didn't need to say anything more. Amore might not make it.

Moisture immediately pooled heavily at the inside corners of my eyes. I'm trying desperately not to let the tears flow. My Amore? Our little girl who so loves life, was going to lose hers due to a bone? I wasn't prepared for this. I wasn't going to be able to say good-bye to her? Malcolm, having to deal with "this" by himself.

My thoughts turned to cutting short my attendance at the convention, getting a flight back to New Mexico, being there for Malcolm, being there for Amore. Being home.

The next words I hear are, "gotta go, the vet's here! I'll call you back when I know more." Malcolm cuts the call. Silence. Dead silence.

Reality hits. It hits hard. I'm a thousand miles away while one of my "kids" was experiencing a life and death medical emergency. Malcolm and I don't have children. We have dogs. Our dogs are our kids. We don't stock up on Cheerios or Fruit Loops, we buy bones and peanut butter. Our cupboards are filled with dog treats and canine kibbles. The toy bin is filled with Kongs, bones and tug-of-war ropes. My little girl wasn't going to make it.

Guilt immediately set in. A bone? A bone was going to be the cause of Amore's death. We had given all of our girls' beef and buffalo bones for years. Bones were the perfect baby-sitter, or in our case, puppy-sitter. We gave our girls bones to gnaw on while we ran into town and run errands. We gave them bones to pacify their chewing tendencies. We gave them bones to keep them quiet. To keep them from destroying the house.

A beef bone given to the dogs meant the house would be intact when we returned home. No chewed library books, no masticated shoes scattered out in the dog pen, no drooled on socks randomly spread from one end of the house to the other, touting new holes in the toes and heels. The girls would be so entranced with their bones, they wouldn't even know we had left home.

Bones were our puppy sitter of choice. And cheap! A few dollars spent on bones kept the house clean and kept the tartar on their teeth to a minimum. Instead of a toy hamper, we had a bone basket, tucked in a corner of the living room.

Each evening the girls would dig through their bone bin, searching for a "good" bone to gnaw on for the night. For the dogs, gnawing on a bone at night was equivalent to sipping on a Cognac at the end of the day. A way to unwind. A way to relax.

Each morning, I would round up the stray bones, scattered about, and put them back in the big wooden bucket. A bone had brought Amore so much enjoyment and now was causing her so much pain. My heart ached.

The second-hand on my watch spun into minutes. Those minutes seemed like hours. I was paralyzed, sitting on the conference hall bench, waiting for Malcolm to call me back, praying for Amore to pull through, for some miracle to occur. It was seventy-eight minutes later before I knew anything more.

Another call and Malcolm apprised me our options were not good, we were running out of time. Ideally, the vet would like to push the bone down into the stomach cavity and then perform surgery to remove it. Stomach surgery is an easier operation than going in through the throat. Berners have a longer throat passage than most large breeds and the vet didn't have a long enough apparatus to force the bone through the tight esophagus.

Worse case scenario: If left too long, the bone will adhere to the esophagus, restricting Amores' breathing, eventually suffocating her.

Second worse case scenario would be to operate in Amore's current state, slicing through the esophagus to reach the stuck bone – the success rate of this type of surgery is very low. Few animals recover from the surgery. Malcolm and I were sitting like lame ducks in the cross hairs of Amore's death. We had run out of options and time.

Another hour had passed, another sixty minutes and still I hadn't moved off the bench. Waiting. Waiting for anything, any word at all.

A text came through from Malcolm, *"goin n 4 srgry. dont fly 2 ABQ. horse vet fix bone. will call u L8r."*

What the hell? Horse vet? What horse vet? Which surgery? The worse case scenario surgery or the ideal surgery? New questions swirled, impatiently waiting to be answered. Sifting through the next few conversations with Malcolm explained Amore's situation.

As Amore was being prepped for esophagus surgery, a large animal veterinarian, just by chance, happened to stop by the clinic. He suggested to the attending veterinarian to try a tool used on equines, allowing him to push the bone down. A tool longer than what the clinic had on hand.

The device was long enough to thread through Amore's throat and down through the esophagus to reach the bone, gently tapping the bone into the stomach. Once the bone was pushed into Amore's stomach, the location of the surgery quickly switched from the throat/esophagus to her belly.

Hallelujah! We had our miracle!

Amore breezed through surgery with a newly shaved tummy, over twenty-five plus staples and a coarse cough due to her throat being constricted, stretched and scratched. We had our little girl back.

We had orders to feed her soft food and keep her quiet. Quiet? Our Amore, who has two speeds, fast and faster? Amore, who is our ADHD dog? We had our work cut out for us but we didn't care. We had our Amore back.

I flew home as scheduled. I asked Malcolm to drive straight from the airport to the vet clinic so I could see Amore. I needed reassurance that Amore was really okay and would recover from her ordeal.

We brought her home the next day and managed to keep her quiet for one more day after that. Two days later you would never know she came so close to dying.

We fired our perfect dog bone baby-sitter that very day. We threw away every bone we could find. Even went out to the pen to dig up any additional bones we could. Malcolm and I forbid any more bones back in the house. The empty bone basket has been moved into the garage. There is no evidence left.

Amore has completely recovered from her ordeal.

Malcolm and I, well… I don't think any parent ever totally recovers when one of their precious kids has a medical emergency.

Today? Let's just say, we smile when we come upon a dog-chewed book or missing shoes.

THE MUTT MOBILE

Mutt mobile. Canine car. Pooch Pick-up. Datsun Dog. Honda Hound. Berner Bus. All names we've christened our more mature automobiles throughout the years. Cars and SUVs that have seen happier days, and in the days before dogs, cleaner ones.

Our first mutt mobile was a grey Chevy Blazer with customized *MAGPIE* license plates. Magpie was a nickname my father gave me at the young age of three. I was a talker. I would warble throughout our family dinner, never taking a pause or a breath. Just like the Magpie, I was a chatterbox.

When I turned twenty-one, my father surprised me with custom license plates for my birthday. Since then, whenever I traded for a new car, I transferred the plates to my new vehicle. Every new car of mine was named Magpie.

MAGPIE moved us to the high desert of New Mexico, carrying Thugs, 1,300 miles from California. It hauled all of our "crap" (my husband's indelicate description of my valued heirlooms). It cleaned up real nice, handled the road well, got decent gas mileage, and was just an' all-round good ol' car. It was the bomb!

When we brought Tiamo into our family, MAGPIE turned into our puppy Porsche. At 10 years old, ol' MAGPIE was still stylish.

The scratches from Tiamo leaping on the car door were, at first, barely visible. We rubbed out the little dents and blemishes. What's a little dog hair along the floorboard, we'd vacuum it another time. The broken vent for the back AC went undetected for several weeks, as did the cracked cup holder and the chewed middle seat belt. MAGPIE still purred softly when on the road.

Malcolm and I both ignored the paw prints and teeth marks that perforated the back leather seats – it added character, we said. The fuse blew out on the passenger door window from Tiamo hitting, and holding, the up/down button with her paws. The overhead dome light cover had disappeared months earlier, no telling where. All fixable, all replaceable and all re-breakable. It was just cosmetics we told ourselves. The structure of MAGPIE was still good as new. MAGPIE was a good car. She had good bones.

Slowly, over time, and with assistance from Tiamo, MAGPIE's age started to show. When the little pups arrived, MAGPIE was turned into the Berner Bus, hauling eight squirming, wiggly Bernese Mountain Dog puppies to and fro the vet clinic for their shots.

As the litter whittled down to Amore and Dolce, along with Tiamo, MAGPIE was known strictly as the dog car. Each dog had their spot: Dolce riding shotgun on my lap in the front passenger seat. Tiamo in the middle back where she could have the air conditioning full blast on her face. Amore on the back driver's side seat, one paw on the window sill.

Pealing paint, ripped leather seats, and a cracking dashboard, in dog years MAGPIE had already turned eighty-four and was quickly heading towards ninety-one. She was a good car. Got us where we needed to go, was mostly reliable, and was the perfect dog car.

After years of hauling Tiamo and the girls around, the interior was trashed, covered in dog hair and reeked of dog smell. There were many non removable dog stains. As the car aged, we no longer stressed about its appearance. So what about a little dog vomit? It was a dog car.

MAGPIE hauled everything from dogs, dirt, to life's paraphernalia. MAGPIE lugged home purchases from Home Depot, carried plants and fertilizer from the Garden Center and the recyclables to the county dump.

It was no longer the car you took to the airport to pick up family and visiting guests. Nor was it the vehicle used to invite co-workers out to lunch. You didn't even really want to go grocery shopping or drive it to go out to dinner. The golden chariot had lost it's shine.

When the government came out with the "Cash for Clunkers" program, we jumped at the opportunity to scrap it. MAGPIE, our precious dog car was worth more dead than alive. It was time to give MAGPIE a proper burial. We started shopping for a new car.

We needed to trade in MAGPIE for a more "economical" vehicle. Since I'm on the road, driving so much, we needed a car that had good gas mileage. Yet still, we needed something that we could load up with our dogs. We needed another dog car.

Our criteria for our next auto purchase was simple. Our new car needed to hold three large dogs. Three hundred pounds of canine. We started the search for another pooch pick-up.

Nothing is worse than car shopping. Dealing with car salesmen, dealing with those vultures that stand on the "point" waiting for buyers to pull in to the dealership. The contest between salesmen: who can get to us first as we are climbing out of the car. No doubt about it, car shopping ranks right up there with having a tooth pulled.

As the salesman was pointing out the wonderful features of the car, Malcolm and I were only concerned if the girls would fit in the back. What we wanted to know is if the girls would be comfortable in the back. We wanted to see how the back seat folded and how much headroom there was. Would they have a back air-conditioner? Would they enter/exit the vehicle through the side doors or from the back hatch? Vinyl or leather seats? Leather will be wrecked in a short matter of time due to paw damage. Vinyl is cheaper.

We thought we were looking for an economical vehicle with good gas mileage to purchase, but in reality we were really looking for another dog car.

We looked at every SUV there was. We drove every type of Subaru, Chevy, Ford, Toyota, Honda, Jeep, Kia, and Dodge available in our area. We put down more back seats than we could count. We measured the height of floor to ceiling in every vehicle we were interested in.

We bought a Prius. Not even close to being able to haul three hundred pound dogs. Good for the environment, not so for our dogs.

But still, we needed a dog car – and sadly, that meant we had to designate our SUV Pilot as the next Honda Hound. We're at the dog hair on the floorboard stage.

HOUDINI

Bernese Mountain Dogs are the type of dog that want to be with you, always. Where you goeth, they goeth. They are not a dog breed to be left on their own for long periods of time.

Bernese Mountain Dogs need and command lots and lots of human companionship and should be considered a full member of the family. They are a wonderful family type dog but if you own a Berner, plan on enjoying them all the time, they are not a breed to be ignored!

If you step outside, they want to be outside with you. If you need to run to the store, they need, no, strike that, they demand to go along with you, riding shotgun in the passenger seat. They will be out the door and in the car before you've begun to search for your car keys.

If you need to visit the restroom, they want to follow you. Walk into the kitchen and paws pitter-patter beside you. Two perpetual furry shadows, dogging your step. Shutting the door on their noses only produces sniffing and scratching, amplified by two.

On occasion we elect to keep the girls home. In the summer, the temperatures are too hot for them to be left in the stuffy car without air conditioning and other times, our errands run longer than we want to keep them cooped up in the SUV. They don't like it. Mostly, they hate it. The Berners consider a peanut butter filled Kong a poor replacement for their human family.

Four hours is about the maximum Malcolm and I feel comfortable in leaving the girls alone, to their own devices and that is only in extreme situations. Any longer than that and we take the risk of a destroyed household.

Dolce and Amore have learned when they may join us for a car ride and when they are staying put, depending on the time of day, the clothes and shoes worn, and if they hear a certain jingle of the car keys.

Early mornings they recognize its "me leaving for work" time. They follow me into the bathroom and hang out while I am getting ready for work. They walk with me to get the morning paper and follow me around as I pour my "must-have" coffee.

By the time I grab my purse and car keys to drive into town for work, they are already sprawled out, napping from their busy morning. As I scratch their ears good-bye, they'll lift their heads, watching me walk out the door, and then they are back in slumber land before I've even pulled out of the garage.

The girls have become highly skilled at learning the difference between a "slide your foot into a sling-back heel" shoe or a "bend over to tie the laces of your hiking boot" shoe. Flip-flops are a no-brainer, the folks are going swimming.

With the sling-back, they are accepting of their fate. Knowing they will be staying home with Gordita, Dolce and Amore have already gone back to what they were doing. Flip-flops equates to mom and dad are going swimming and will return smelling of chorine. Uck! The boot means "WALK," "RIDE," or "BOTH." All of which creates pandemonium, with all hell breaking out.

They can interpret the tinkling of keys in three notes or less. A jingle of the car keys will bring, a head lift to decipher the key jingle code, causing a quick tilt of the head, a twitch of the ear, listening for the right key clink.

A quick "come on, Girls!" will jump start a concerto of joyous high-pitched barking that continues through the process of loading them into the vehicle, should the girls be so lucky as to join us.

To our ever living dismay, Malcolm and I have discovered there are times when Dolce and Amore have attempted to follow us, ignoring our command to stay put, watching over the house when we are away.

On one such time, I drove home from work to find Dolce and Amore contained in the front portal, the front door wide open. They burst out into excited barks as I turned into our driveway, excited mom was home. I assumed Malcolm had opened the door for fresh air, creating a cross-breeze through the sun-warmed house, not thinking at all about using caution as I entered.

"Honey, I'm home!" I called out as I entered through the garage door. Silence. All was quiet on the human front.

"Hon?" I questioned, as I walked further into the house. No answer. Both the front and the back door wide open. Where the hell could he be, I wondered? A full glass of his southern iced tea sitting on the end table hadn't even started to condense. It was obvious he was around somewhere.

In reality, Malcolm had walked next door to deliver some misplaced mail, thinking he would only be gone a few minutes. The girls, listening to the crunch of gravel as Malcolm walked up the driveway, hated the idea of being left alone at home, for however short a time.

In her essential need to be with Malcolm, Dolce had pawed the dead bolt, scratching and marking the back-side of our thick, wooden front door with her claws. Finally unlocking the dead bolt, on the downswing, her paws hit the door handle, swinging the door wide open.

Freedom was theirs. Thankfully, the half-walls of the front portal are too high for them to jump over and escape, plus the gate was fully closed. They were safe inside our protected front garden area, but they had just become well schooled in breaking and exiting.

Dolce is a quick learner. That one time flight of escape was all she needed to learn the "how-to-unlock-doors" trick. Our closet door was next on the list to practice on. Then she moved on to the back door.

Dolce turned her clever door-opening talent to other doors throughout the house. Back doors, garage doors, closet doors, cabinet doors, even shower doors, she opens and shuts doors like a cat burglar professional. No door is sacred. No door is safe.

Dolce stands on her hind legs and uses her front paws to turn the dead-bolt lock. She then uses her weight to push in the door, gaining entry into the next room. Should the door shut on her, Dolce will repeat the process, and with a descending slide, she hooks her paws on the handle lever and pulls towards her body to open the door and come back through. Our girl is a smart and clever dog.

Twice, while at work, I've received frantic phone calls from Terri, our next door neighbor reporting the girls were out wandering the neighborhood. Malcolm had left the dogs at home while he ran into town for some errands. Consequently, Dolce and Amore had tried to follow Malcolm, not wanting to be left alone.

Dolce's special talent of escape has had me leaving work in a urgent rush to get home to find the two rascals. By the time I pull into the driveway, they have heard my car engine and are running to greet me. Happy to have mom home.

At two in the morning, we will awake to hear the slamming of the door to the garage as Dolce patrols through the house during the night.

I call it her security check. Dolce does a walk through, doing her rounds, then a few minutes later, we'll hear the door slam again when Dolce enters back into our abode. And all we need to do is feed her. Cheap.

Malcolm calls it the cat box circuit. Dolce checking for ucky stuff to eat out of the litter box. We will then hear the clicking of her nails as she comes back into the bedroom to her dog pillow. With a deep sigh, she is asleep in seconds.

We caution our over-night guests to lock their bedroom door or they might have a four-legged caller greet them during the middle of the night. Dog or cat, we never know. We encourage visitors to please lock the bathroom door behind them or they might have Dolce with them, along with a wide open door.

Dolce's skills has forced Malcolm to take stronger measures against future door openings. We've installed additional hardware, slide locks and hooks, key locks and more dead bolts, all designed to keep our canine Houdini hound where she belongs. Placed well above her paw reach, we have avoided any more door-opening tricks.

She still tries. Dolce still wants to be with us. She still wants our company. Where we goeth, she wants to go.

Scratch marks adorn several of our household doors. The front door has been refinished twice. The molding around the closet door has been replaced and the rubber weather seal surrounding the garage door frame has been ripped to shreds. Three times.

I am thankful this door opening proficiency isn't genetic and Amore isn't that smart! But then, maybe she is – Dolce is the one opening the door for her.

TAIL THUMPING

Thump.

Thump. Thump.

Thump-thump-thump.

Thump-thump-thumpity-thump.

Whack! Whack-whack! Whack! C.R.A.S.H.

It starts out slow. Thump. Thump. It builds up to a deafening whackity-whack explosion. It ends with major collateral damage done between the tail and the inanimate object it is hitting and hammering.

Knowing the difference between a one thump tail thunk and a whackity-whack wallop can rescue dog owners from future calamity. Knowing the difference between a steady beat of a canine's tail and a heavy trouncing of a dog's rudder can liberate an owner from mayhem and mishap.

Here are descriptive clues on what each dog tail-thump and whackity-whack really mean....

The ol' one tail-thump given by a dog, is clearly an insult to its human caregiver. The slightest lift of their head, barely acknowledging something might be happening, perhaps an arch of the brow or a twitch of the ear is an affront to its owner. The one tail-thump is the rudest of all thumps.

Dolce is an expert at one thumps. She won't move off the couch unless there is value in it for her. She'll lift her head, arch her brow, and maybe, just maybe she'll twitch her ear, listening, watching, waiting to see what's a' happening. Then decide the effort to investigate isn't worth the energy of moving from her dog bed of comfort and lethargy.

Malcolm and I have been ignored. This is good. We can return to whatever we were doing.

A two or three and perhaps a four tail-thump is an improvement. Thump. Thump. Thump. Her curiosity has been aroused, but she is still unsure of the appeal. Dolce has now expanded enough energy to give Malcolm and I several beats of interest before emitting a loooong drawn out sigh.

One eye ajar, wavering between going back to sleep or exploring this new development, this multi tail-thumper is classified as a true put-upon sign of disgruntlement.

Dolce really doesn't want to get up to probe, to investigate, but she also doesn't want to miss anything. So far so good. We're safe. We have a 90% chance her dog dreams are more important than rising to sniff out her curiosity. We go back to doing what we were doing.

Now a thumpity-thump-thump-thump is heading into the danger zone. This is a totally different story. Dolce's tail speed is kicking up, creating 30 mph winds. Eyes alert, standing at attention, Dolce's interest has been piqued. We've got 100 pounds of torque just waiting for the secret, silent signal to move. Problem is, we don't know what the secret, silent signal might be.

Humans beware, be on the look out, be ready. The difference between a three tail thump and a thumpity thump is beyond anything you can imagine. Let those cookies burn in the oven. MOVE. You need to divert disaster before it attacks you. The odds have swung in a new direction and have swiftly advanced up to a solid 83% chance of Rapid Canine Involvement (RCI). Pay attention. Do. Not. Turn. Your. Back. On. Tail. You are on the runway to lift off with your canine gaining lift and speed. Danger. Danger. Pay attention!

When Dolce decides to join the fray, her tail is the first thing we look for. Wildly thumping to the right, she is getting ready to approach. Though not all tail thumps are created equal, a right side swinging tail thump is a good sign. Supposedly, dogs respond to the direction of a tail wag. Canines that thump their tails to the right are looking at something they want to approach, such as their owner. They will wag their tails to the left when confronted with something they want to back away from, such as another dog with an aggressive posture.

Left or right, this brings us to the tail whack. There are two distinct tail whacks that dog owners need to pay attention to. The whack and the whackity-whack. Simple.

The single whack entails moving the iced tea glass from the tail's trajectory path. Safe enough? Or is it?

Tail whacks are stronger than thumps, even thumpity thumps. The whack's strength comes from the tail's speed and velocity. Its power lies in the unexpectedness, the surprise of the ambush, the suddenness of the whack.

A Dolce whack can bring about a shattered glass. It can send a cell phone flying 15 feet. It can cause a dust-devil twirl-wind, spreading havoc and destruction throughout our house with books and papers spewed all over the floor. It can cause pain. It can bruise. It can hurt. Her whackity-whack can put you on 24 hour bed rest.

Dolce's whackity-whack tail whack would put TSA on red alert. Whacks of this type will inevitably bring a loud, vociferous collision of canine tail and object. Be cautious. Be very careful.

Dolce's tail whacking at this velocity can literally cause annihilation of your home. This whack is a weapon of mass destruction. Not only is Dolce excited, but her tail is way past the stimulation phase. It is incited with power, speed and motivation.

Decorative couch pillows have known to blow up, millions of little white feathers spreading like wildfire throughout the house. Coffee cups shattered in one swoop of a frantic whackity-whack. Newspapers, mail and file folders flown into the air, scattering like blind mice on the run. Whackity whacks are a force of nature.

Do not call 911.

You are on your own here. At this point, you are totally screwed. If you have any cookies left that aren't burnt, I'd start eating. This is a chocolate situation.

KITCHEN CLATTER

With the loud swoosh of the refrigerator door opening, Tiamo, Amore and Dolce are immediately on high alert to any possible kitchen activity. Their bodies tense in hopeful waiting, their noses lifted high as they attempt to determine exactly what is happening in the kitchen.

The clink of condiment jars rattling against each other as the door swings open usually will inform the girls of a nibble of something tasty. The crinkling of plastic is blatant advertising of either a cheese crumble or maybe a carrot stick, signaling to the girls to head into the kitchen, something good is about to happen.

To the dogs, the un-snapping of a plastic lid translates to yogurt or sour cream. All of which equals to a chance of a tasty treat. The three of them are at the ready.

If the girls happen to be in the living room, they will climb up on the highest peak, usually the couch, front paws on the back straining over the end tables to see what's going on. Back paws on the seat cushion for height, three tri-colored dog snouts crinkling and sniffing as they investigate the scents in the air pouring from the refrigerator, wafting out of the kitchen.

If they are residing in other parts of the house, before the fridge door has had a chance to snap closed, all three of them are in the kitchen, overly confident a flavorsome treat will fall to the floor for them to grab.

They all have heard the fridge door open, the swoosh suction sounds traveling throughout the house. It's an all-out race between the three, who can sprint to the kitchen the fastest, nosing out the others for a dropped delicacy. Muzzles to the floor, they are in the "get-it-before-the-others" mode.

From as far as the living room, the girls can decipher if the clanking reverberations are Malcolm reaching into the refrigerator to grab his pitcher of iced tea or if the crackling sound is some cheddar cheese being placed on the kitchen counter for slicing or grating. Iced tea, they will sit back down. A hint of cheese and they are in the kitchen under foot within a nano second, hoping for a bite. The three of them all sitting on their haunches, confident Malcolm or I will submit to their begging. Not!

They can identify and verify the different noises of the fridge door and the freezer, knowing the different hums and swooshes between the two. Freezer doors don't even merit a lift of their brow. Fridge doors have more importance, more value to their tummy, therefore fridge doors have the distinction of ranking higher on the interest scale.

They can confirm the dissimilarity between the lifting of their doggy treat jar lid and our spare change crock cover, between the squeak of the cupboard and the screech of the utensil drawer. It is only the jangle of the treat jar lid that will bring them running.

Their ears can define a broccoli chop vs. an onion cut, a carrot slice vs. celery stick. The sound of the knife against the chopping block as it cuts through the various veggies announces how quickly the girls will start sniffing around the kitchen. They love broccoli and carrots, can't have onions, and are so-so with celery. Forget about bell peppers and cauliflower, neither has any calling power.

With any kitchen clamor, Amore will immediately run in to investigate. Nose to the floor, sniffing out the latest crumb, Amore is determined to lick up any fallen treasure before Dolce or Tiamo has a chance.

Now, Tiamo had the patience of Job. She would willingly wait out the kids, knowing she'll get a nibble or two just for being Tiamo. She knew, as it was her due, that she would be given a treat, no matter what. Personally, hand-delivered straight to her jaws. There is no need for her to hustle into the kitchen, as she brings up the rear. She was the presiding matriarch. Queen dogs always gets first dibs on eats.

Dolce, on the other hand, is more discerning. She'll wait on the couch, head tilted, eyebrows cocked, listening. Her little mind working to interpret the sounds coming from the scullery, she postpones leaving the couch until she knows for sure there is appropriate enticement. She wants to know the clatter is worth the effort of movement, that the crackling of packaging is worth the energy to cruise into the gallery. But once she hears Amore crunching down on a green bean stem, she's right there wanting her share.

The jingle jangle of the silverware drawer won't even merit a head lift from her soft pillow on the couch. Neither will the slam of the cupboard or the thump of the microwave door as it's being shut. However, the scent of an apple wedge, a cheese cube or a carrot stick will haul Dolce off the divan and into the kitchen in three seconds flat. If she hears Amore chomping a broccoli stalk, she can be there in two. If Tiamo starts to amble within snout grabbing range of the kitchen boundaries, Dolce is on her tail, not to be left out.

I would have to say cheese is their absolute favorite. Even Bleu Cheese. Broccoli and green beans are tied for second and Chobani low-fat pineapple yogurt comes in third. During the summer months, Dolce craves fruit. Come September and October she switches to pumpkins and apples.

Don't expect the girls to sit patiently if the cheese cube or broccoli stock falls on the floor, quietly waiting for permission to go after the dropped delicacy. Crumbs on the floor are a free for all.

If something does tumble to the floor, it only brings pandemonium. Three muzzles searching out the treasure. Three snouts sniffing out where the treat landed. Three determined canines competing with each other to find the fallen extravagance.

Do not get in their way!

SIBLING RIVALRY

Siblings. Most of us have them. Most of us love them. Now. Perhaps not so much when we were younger.

When we are 10 years old, our older and/or younger brothers and sisters are the bane of our existence. The natural pecking order decrees: the older sibs pick on us, and the youngest ones, by nature of being the littlest, bug us. Those in the middle are stuck.

Hopefully by the time we are a legal adult, those same unbearable siblings, those unbearable beasts and brats, are our best friends.

The years in between, the years sandwiched between ten and twenty are layered with childish fights over who is Granny's favorite, who got the bigger slice of apple pie and cries of "am-so-am-not!"

These adolescent years are peppered with fights and spats over who received better grades, scored higher on a test and was most popular at school.

Throughout is the underlying rivalry of 'besting them'; a thin whisper of competitiveness is threaded between and around siblings, to do just as well, if not better. To out-score, out-smart and out-win that older beast of a sibling from our younger years.

Though poles apart in personality, talent and smarts, Amore and Dolce do share one thing in common – sibling rivalry. Between the two of them, they are always trying to "out-do" the other.

Believe you me, they know if they have been slighted. If one receives an extra indulgent treat over the other. When the other is benefiting from special attention. Whether or not they have been left behind from a trip in the car. They know. Boy, do they know!

Dogs have an innate ability to know if they have been snubbed. They know if they have been insulted. Even if they have a right to be affronted. Retaliation is their only recourse, and I can assure you, they will retaliate. One way or another, they will get their due. Beware!

Their sibling competitiveness kicks into high gear as they jockey for position to sit next to Malcolm or myself on the couch for their nighttime loving. Their rivalry over who gets to sit besides Malcolm or me is an all-out war with the couch as the battle field. Me as the prize. To the victor goes the spoils. Happy only if they think they have out-maneuvered the other. I'm not sure if they really want to sit by me or if they just want to block the other from having the joy of snuggling. Whatever the case, the battle takes place with me in the middle.

Dolce likes to back into the pocket between the couch pillows and my side, scooting closer and closer against me. Amore likes to come around by the back of the sofa to divide, separate and conquer.

Jealousy takes over if one of the girls is getting all the petting and belly rubs. Nose nudging our elbow to disrupt the canine massage. They will maneuver their furry head up and under our elbow, stealing some ear-scratching pleasure away from the other.

In the mean time, the one receiving the love, tries to hold your forearm down with their front paws, clutching your wrist so you are unable to scratch, itch, pet or rub their sibling. It doesn't matter their own belly rub has stopped, their only concern is keeping the other from getting a little pat, a little love.

All of a sudden Dolce and Amore are mathematicians, counting the exact number of kibbles given out. Counting down to the last treat given, and to whom, they know if an additional delicious golden nugget was dropped and caught by the other. They know if the other has landed an extra Milk Bone. Amore knows if Dolce received two treats to her one. Dolce recognizes if any injustice has befallen to her.

On leash, Amore takes the lead, her nose just inches past Dolce's, but ahead none the least. Going to the store, Dolce is riding shotgun no matter what, no matter at what cost.

Between the two of them, they are always trying to out-do the other. Amore can out-run, out-race her sis. Dolce out-smarts and out-wits her litter mate.

On occasion, we'll hear a low growl, the start of a sibling squabble, resulting in a pout from Amore or a yelp from Dolce. Just as quick, it's forgotten, the toy ignored.

Today, Amore and Dolce are best buddies, side by side. They share their food but not their treats. Amore pulls ahead on walks, Dolce grabs the front seat on car trips.

Both can do the math.

MINE

Grrrrrrrrr!

Mine!

Do.

Not.

Even.

Think.

About.

It.

Whether it's a shoe, a bone or a precious peanut butter filled Kong, the treasure becomes more valuable when you have possession... and, fair game to all others who don't. The old adage, "Possession is nine-tenth ownership" doesn't mean squat to Dolce or Amore.

One of Dolce's favorite past-times is chewing on her Kong. If there is still peanut butter inside, all the better. She'll carry her Kong from room to room to room, as she follows us around the house.

Dolce will tuck it under her front paws for additional security. If Amore gets too close for comfort, a low growl of warning tumbles from deep inside her throat.

"Back away and stay away!" Dolce repeats the warning. Little good it does. Amore just waits in the theatre wings for her opportunity to steal the Kong. Her chance will come. Just wait. Amore waits for her cue to steal the Kong.

If the cone-shaped rubber Kong happens to slip out from Dolce's grasp, awkwardly rolling under some piece of furniture, she'll spend several minutes digging it out. Desperate to retrieve the Kong before Amore can lay claim to it.

She'll wiggle under the couch, as much as a 100 pound deep-barrel chested Bernese Mountain Dog can wiggle, her nose buried, paw extended, the Kong just out of her reach.

She'll back out from underneath and scramble to another side of the sofa, and try another approach. Looking at her Kong dilemma from all angles, she tries once more to extract her prized possession.

Dolce is our thinker. Head tilted, she is always trying to solve the puzzle. Always trying to crack the code and unravel the mystery. Dolce dives back under the couch for a second attempt to retrieve her Kong. The third try has Dolce backing out from under the leather couch.

A huff and a puff later, and she is squirming out from under the sofa, sending us a beseeching look, head tilted, silently begging us to assist her in recovering her toy.

"Please?" she pleads with her gentle doe eyes. If she can't get the Kong from down under, she knows Mom or Dad will. One of us will eventually get down on the hard bricks and grab her Kong.

"Pulleeese!" Dolce begs once more, her soft brown eyes imploring either Malcolm or myself to assist her in rescuing her beloved Kong. Confident one of us will help her, she gives us her head tilt as she sits on her haunches. She bats her eyes. I did tell you the girls are simply irresistible.

"Now! Before Amore gets it!" She is insistent, desperate in her attempt to get her toy. Her right front paw stroking our leg, determined we will get her Kong before Amore gets involved in the retrieval. It's hard to resist such anxious dispair.

Losing the coin toss to see who will crawl on their hands and knees to locate the Kong, it's my unlucky turn. I wiggle on my stomach, cheek against the cold brick floor attempting to flush out the Kong from under the sofa. Malcolm stands back to watch. Personally, I think he just wanted to check out my bum being up in the air.

Having to incorporate a long wooden handle of a broom to sweep the Kong out from under the sofa, Dolce supervises my attempts from her perch on top of the couch. She, of course, is eagerly anticipating the return of her favorite rubber toy.

About this time Amore becomes interested in the ownership of the Kong. She waits patiently for the tide to change. She is confident her turn to have possession is coming. Eyes alert, Amore waits her chance.

As I said, "Possession is nine-tenths ownership" and Amore wants possession. She barrels her way into the fray to steal the Kong away from Dolce just as I use the broom to brush the Kong out from under the couch. The Kong awkwardly orbits out from its hiding place.

It's a fast line drive to left field. Amore grabs the Kong on its first bounce to freedom. Held strongly in her jaws, Amore immediately dances a jubilant jig. Her happy dance. Her "I've got it, you don't" dance. Her main objective is to antagonize Dolce with it.

Like a typical sibling, Amore parades her major league catch in front of Dolce, holding the stolen loot in her clenched jaws, taunting Dolce with the prize.

"Na na nan na na!" Amore torments Dolce with the Kong.

Dolce barks her frustration at losing her Kong.

"Give it back!" Dolce barks. Still barking, she frantically paces from one end of the couch to the other, tracking Amore as she continues to add injury to insult to Dolce.

Pillows start to fly off the couch, Dolce is getting into position to leap across the ottoman to lunge at Amore. Amore is still gripping the Kong. Chaos is about to be unleashed!

Now just imagine, you are still lying on your stomach, the cold brick floor against your bare skin, broom handle still in hand. Imagine you are just beginning to inch your way out from under the sofa. Scooting out so you can stand up, belly off the floor.

Now imagine, Amore stepping on your lower back and legs as she continues to needle and antagonize her canine sibling. Paws digging into your back. Pacing back and forth as she holds the Kong. Every fifth pace, she lands a paw on the your back, her claws digging into your exposed skin. You have another hundred pound dog, Dolce, whose barking has intensified into a loud frenzy, a nano second away from flying across your prone form to start a well-deserved Kong attack against Amore. Yikes!

Imagine, in your effort to crawl out from under the couch, you try to stand at the exact moment Dolce takes the first shot, jumping towards Amore to retrieve her Kong.

At this point there is no more imagination, it's for real! Yep! I am in the middle a Kong fight, buried under eight paws and two hundred pounds of sumo wrestling sisters, contesting canines, battling it out for the glory of red rubber, and perhaps a little left-over peanut butter.

I fall backwards, landing on my arse, as two large dogs are on top of me, struggling over a Kong. Paws and claws punching my limbs and torso, I'm flat on my back, pushed back into the unforgiving bricks.

No defense. No protection. No help from Malcolm, he's off to the sidelines laughing his ass off over my predicament. One hand on the broom handle, the other trying to push off the first felonious canine I can. I shove off one dog. Sounds of laughter coming from the background as my husband is bent over at the waist from laughing too hard.

"STOP!" I scream, nursing my injured bum with one hand. Slowly raising from the floor, Dolce and Amore look at me with surprise.

"Who us?" Dolce and Amore both angle their heads in question, their soft reddish-brown brows raised in query.

"What did we do?" The fight all but forgotten. The precious Kong laying on the hard floor, ignored and now ancient history. There is truth in the statement that dogs live in the moment. The fight over, the Kong forgotten. Ancient history. Over and done.

I grabbed the offending Kong and placed it on the top of the refrigerator. High enough that Dolce and Amore can't reach it, but just on the edge so they both can see it and know it is up there.

Out of reach. Tantalizing them. I have my own way of getting back at them!

Dolce and Amore have a running tally of who has stolen, swiped, taken, nabbed, grabbed, pilfered, filched, snatched, pinched, nicked and all out fought for, the red rubber prize out from under an unsuspecting muzzle.

Amore is slightly ahead in steals, Dolce leads in cunning rebounds.

Malcolm and I surrender.

MUST LOVE DOG.... HAIR!

When Malcolm and I married, we knew we wanted to move out of California, only we didn't know exactly where.

My only condition: it had to be west of the Mississippi, leaving us a large section on the left side of the map to pick from. Malcolm's only stipulation: our new home had to have home-delivery of the New York Times, which narrowed it down quite a bit.

There are miles of rural areas west of the Mississippi that to this day does not receive the NY Times – not even a Starbucks to shill out some dollars for the Times. Our search for a new home tapered drastically down to specialized areas.

The dart landed on Santa Fe, New Mexico, a southwest tourist mecca located in the high desert of Northern New Mexico. Tucked up tight against the Sangre de Cristos Mountain Range, Santa Fe plays host to a wide range of cultures, has many museums, and boasts some great restaurants. There is a wide variety of outdoor sports and adventures, and lots of shopping opportunities. You'll find everything from expensive art and Indian jewelry to cheap T-shirts with silk-screened scenes depicting the Southwest.

Santa Fe has all the advantages of a large metropolitan city and yet holds all the charm and benefits of a smaller town. Claiming a population of around 70,000, Santa Fe is not only the county seat but is also the State capital of New Mexico.

We went all in. Changed our zip code and moved to New Mexico.

The lure of Santa Fe brings thousands of visitors annually. It also brings lots of family and friends to our household. Guests who arrive for mini get-away vacations. Friends stopping through while attending a conference or business meetings in our City Different. Chums and pals escaping for a few days from their hectic lives. When you live in a popular port-of-call, friends of the past find you. Friends you didn't even know you had are now your BFF.

While we happily open the doors of our home, welcoming our friends and family, we always feel the need to preface their visit with a few kind words of warning.

MUST LOVE DOGS......

AND DOG HAIR!

And a very fat cat named Gordita.

What we really mean is, visitors and guests must love **OUR** dogs. AND, not be allergic to cats. And guests must give our beloved menagerie the proper love and attention they so deserve. All of them! Tiamo, Dolce, Amore and Gordita. We find this weeds out the riff raff.

"Pet 'em!" Malcolm encourages our guests. He will then promptly give a quick demonstration on the proper petting techniques. Whether they want to or not, our guests are stuck petting our girls. Malcolm insists on it, the dogs demand it. Gordita tolerates it.

House guests are not allowed to be upset if their kicked off shoes left in the living room end up outside in the dog pen. Nor if they discover they are missing a sock a few days after they go home. Or, if there are clumps of long black dog hair clinging to their pant's leg and to their shirttails and to their jacket and to everything else they own. Nope, house guests have no right to be dismayed or distraught over "a little" dog hair. They were warned.

I remember once getting a call a few days after our visitors had left. "I brought home some dog hair!" was the preamble as I answered the phone. All I could do was laugh.

Throughout their stay, the odds are high our guests will pull a stray strand of dog hair from their wineglass, or see a puff of canine curls floating down and around. There is no doubt, that sometime within their visit, dog hair will become a part of their short stay in Santa Fe.

Malcolm and I chuckle to ourselves when we catch sight of a guest discretely pulling a black dog hair off their gloss coated lips. We giggle over watching friends smooth out their wrinkled pant's leg as they try to dislodge loose fur bits. We secretly smile as we observe them constantly washing their hands after engaging the girls with love. We give each other the eye when we notice a friend pushing one of the girls away from their nicely pressed khakis.

When guests and visitors come to Santa Fe, especially if they stay with us, putting up with dog hair is a pre-requisite. Loving our dogs is a requirement.

We advise our friends to shut their bedroom door tight at night or they could very well end up with one to three animals curled up next to them, and there is a very good possibility of a very fat cat, sharing not only the soft mattress but adding more fur and hair to the mix.

We are on a first name basis at the dry cleaners. We repeatedly wash our bed spreads, even to go as far as purchasing a "spare" spread that we switch out every so often. We regularly invest in lint rollers, and place a roller in every room for convenience. Even I do a roller run-through on my slacks every morning before leaving for work, checking for excess dog hair.

Malcolm and I try to keep the dog hair to a minimum. With three large furry canines in the house, it's a hard task, even with the cost of hiring a housecleaner.

After several years, we have filtered our guest list down to three categories:

Those that LOVE our girls, keeping their bedroom door wide open, hoping for a midnight cuddle and don't mind the stray dog hair. These guests are our favorite. These guests are invited back again;

Those that don't mind our dogs, but don't really want much to do with the dog hair that comes with them. These visitors will give a little pet, a tiny bit of love to the inhabitants of our zoo, but they are careful with their shoes and keep the lint roller in hand. These visitors have a three day window before we politely ask them to move on;

And then there are those friends and family that stay in a hotel.

Enough said.

SUNDAY TRADITION

Monday through Friday, I am the one to get up early to feed the girls their morning meal. Real early. 5:00 a.m. early. Our girls are conditioned to enjoy their breakfast at the crack of dawn, when it's still dark and cold out. When the sun is still hiding behind the blackened mountain range to the east. Five in the freaking morning is an un-godly hour, especially on weekends, but we do it.

The dogs are on a twelve hour feeding schedule. 5:00 a.m. is breakfast. 5:00 p.m. is dinner. Any treat or snack thrown their way in between is their bonus meal. Sort of like free baseball when entering into the tenth inning.

Once their bellies are full, they settle back down on their huge dog pillows for a little morning shut-eye while I continue to get ready for work. As I sip my coffee and read the paper before I leave for work, Tiamo, Dolce and Amore are replenished. They've eaten, therefore, they are happy. Their bellies are full, therefore, they are sated.

Come the weekend, my wonderful, sweet hubby gets up early to feed the girls, allowing me to sleep a couple more hours before I start the day. He'll rise when the little hand hits the 5:00 o'clock mark, tend to the girls, settle them down and then crawl back into bed for more sleep.

For some perverse reason, on the weekends, the dogs start scrambling for their breakfast around 4:00 a.m. waking up waaaay too early for the weekend to start.

They'll come around to the side of the bed, checking to see if one of us is up yet, being sure to whack their tail several times for good measure. On a good day, they might wait until 4:16 a.m. before starting their wake-up antics. If need be, Amore will jump up on the bed and sit on one of us in her attempt to get fed. Checking to see if one of us is awake yet.

It's about this time, I'm kicking Malc in the back, "it's your turn to feed 'em!" I mumble, rolling back over, immediately falling back into slumber land.

Blurry eyed, and three-quarters still asleep, Malcolm stumbles out to the darkened kitchen, tripping over three hundred excited pounds of dog, the combined weight of three hungry dogs in their mad bid for their morning kibbles.

"Crap!" Okay, he really said something a lot stronger but I can't print that. Poor man, my husband isn't a morning person.

From the other room, I hear several more choice words spewing loudly from his lips as his bare feet and legs are clawed by dog paws in their eagerness to be fed.

"Shit! Damn! F%$#K!" He cusses. Loudly. He has probably stepped on a cacti spine one of the girls brought in from outside. I know he just wants to wake me up. So I will give him some sympathy. The girls are happy someone is up. Happier to be fed, but they like knowing someone is around with them. Let's face it, dogs are just happy. Not so much Malcolm.

I hear the clank and clatter from the metal dog bowls being pushed around the hard brick floor as they devour their breakfast. Then quiet. Blissful quiet. Wonderful-fall-back-to-sleep quiet.

While the girls are still chowing down their food, Malcolm crawls back into the still warm bed, staking out his territory on the mattress.

He has about one minute to fluff his down pillows and get comfortable before the girls search us out, done with their breakfast. They climb up on the bed to snuggle in for a few more hours. In the early mornings of the weekend, they like to join us for an hour or so of cuddling.

He has 30 seconds left in his bid to stretch out his legs before Dolce or Amore, or both, steal some of the precious mattress acreage. To stake out his territory before it is gone to the dogs.

He has two seconds left to pull up the covers before the girls plop their weight on top of them, keeping the blankets and bed spread under their bellies and not over Malcolm. It's a race. The starting gun has been fired.

A half hour later, Gordita joins the family snuggle fest, stepping over fur and canine bodies to curl up on a down pillow higher up on the bed, away from Tiamo, Dolce and Amore. Up by our heads, Gordita lays down in a curled up twist, slowly flipping over on her back, showing off her belly, four paws in the air. Her fluffy tail draped over my face.

By the time I'm ready to rise for the day, I have two dogs stretched out on each side of me and a cat up by my pillow loudly purring in my ear. A black cat tail is draped across my cheek just under my nose. I can't move. I can barely breathe. I glance over at Malcolm and see a slight smile forming on his lips, just peaking above the covers, his eyes crinkling at the corners.

Sunday morning is our special day of the week to laze around, read the paper, drink our coffee, share breakfast. It has turned into tradition, having our girls curled up around us as we read the comics, the Op-Ed page, the local news, sipping hot coffee, still in bed, still in our PJs, being careful not to spill any hot coffee on the covers. Breakfast turns into brunch, but who cares, it's our lazy day to enjoy our family.

I can remember as a small child, my sisters and I would climb into bed with our mother on Saturday mornings, dad already up, out and about. One by one, as we woke up, we would troop down the stairs and pitter-pat our way to our parents' bedroom, climbing up on the bed to crawl under the covers.

I think of my mother, her children snuggled against her in the quiet of a Saturday morning. I have no doubt the contentment she felt having all her kids cuddled next to her.

"Psst! You awake?" I persist in waking Malcolm. One visible eye opens, we share a contented, loving look as we take in the sight of our "kids" nestled on the bed. Our family.

It brings a warm hug to our hearts.

CAT FIGHT

The morning was a normal 5:00 a.m. wake-up. Amore lumbered by at her usual time of 4:14 a.m. to press wet wake up doggy kisses on my cheek. Dolce was still on her doggy pillow.

Once Dolce sensed Amore was getting some early morning love, she barreled in between Amore and the side of the bed to ensure her share of early morning ear scratching. Two muzzles up close, each wanting their share of affection.

Like clock-work, the girls followed me through my morning ritual of getting ready for work, eagerly anticipating breakfast once I was finished. About 10 minutes in, Gordita arrived from her where-ever-she-goes-at-night-time-hidey-hole to loudly scratch at the bottom of the bathroom door, determined to be let in to join the early morning soiree.

The three of them, Dolce, Amore and Gordita, quietly lazed about, each curled up in their own special spot on the floor. They were still waking up to their full potential for the day to come. One by one, they took turns in giving me good morning hugs before returning to their corners.

Amore likes to put her front paws on the counter next to me so she can rub her muzzle up against me, receiving a rub in return. She'll nose nudge me under my elbow until I offer a hug, massaging her belly as she stretches from the floor to the counter.

Gordita jumps from the rim of the bath tub to the sink counter and weaves her quiet way softly over hair brushes and a tube of toothpaste to leap onto my shoulder, liking to nuzzle my neck for a few minutes before I set her back down.

Like Tiamo did, Dolce loves to push her way between my legs to get her ears scratched. Shoving me from behind, she pushes until her head pokes through. I reach down to give her some doggy love, rubbing her ears and scratching her neck. All three have been loved and petted.

About the time I'm ready for some hot coffee, Amore and Dolce have fully woken up and are ready for their own breakfast. It's onward to the kitchen. All three animals follow me to the kitchen. Dolce is in the lead as Gordita sprints between dog paws and tails to reach a safe haven under the kitchen table ready to watch the breakfast festivities. I perform the routine procedure of filling their dishes with their kibbles, making the two sit for their meal.

Both Amore and Dolce have learned to sit quickly on their haunches, knowing I won't place the feed bowls down until they have earned it. Side by side, they immediately dive into their respective dog bowls. The two of them have eaten their meals shoulder to shoulder since they were little puppies. Slurps, crunches and the rattle of the tin bowl are the only noises heard.

Once I give them their chow, I grab a flashlight and walk up the drive to retrieve the morning newspaper. By the time I get back to the house, the girls are usually just finishing. Sometimes one will polish off their meal ahead of the other, sometimes they clean their bowls at the same time. But always, once finished, they wander over to where I'm sitting with the paper for a little love, some extra rubs.

Until one morning…..

One morning, those little bitches got into a catfight. I couldn't believe it!

Since they were little tykes, Amore and Dolce have happily enjoyed their meals together, side by side, shoulder to shoulder. They have their own dog bowls, nestled in a raised double-panned stand – Dolce's on the right, Amore's next door on the left. They know which side belongs to whom and line up appropriately.

For over six years, they have received the same portions, the same food, at the same time. Dolce is always the first to sit. Amore is always first to dig in. Until one morning these two big babies started a fight over the last nibble! Six years of peace broken.

It's typical for Amore to finish her meal first and Dolce to lap up hers a close second later. Until, Amore unwisely decided to investigate what was still left in Dolce's bowl and quickly gobbled it up before Dolce could. War broke out. Combat ensued.

Conflict started in the middle of the kitchen with snarls, growls, raised paws and big fangs barred. Holy Guacamole! I've always been told to never get in the middle of a dog fight. To break up the fight, I found a long-handled broom and swatted the behind of the closest dog to me with the bristled end. Hoping a distracted mutt would cease-fire, I turned to the other WFC contender and popped her hinny with another bristled broom punch.

Talk about a little early morning excitement. Their loud and contested dispute brought Malcolm running into the kitchen from a sound slumber, to see me taking my last wallop with the broom and Amore slinking off to her corner to lick her pride.

The hostilities ceased. Truce was called. Phew! The peace treaty was signed.

"What the hell is going on?" Malcolm stumbled into the kitchen.

"Your bitches just got into a big fight!" I replied. I was in shock over the whole incident. I never claim ownership of the dogs when they misbehave. At that point, Malcolm has full title, the mortgage of dog ownership is in his name.

I wanted Malcolm to recognize my sacrifice to enter into the fray, the danger I put myself in. "I had to break them up!" I said to enhance the risk I took, embellishing the peril. Ok, so it wasn't an all-out fight, but it was close. I still needed the broom to stop the riot.

On one hand I was glad to see Dolce stand up for herself. She has always been more docile, even a little timid when it comes to her bossy, overly-confident sis. On the other, I certainly didn't want to have cat fights ensuing every time we fed them.

Suffice to say, the following evening their feed bowls were separated and the broom was kept handy. Peace has reigned ever since.

FETCH AND CATCH

Our dogs do not fetch the newspaper. They do not deliver your fuzzy slippers, nor do they catch the ball. They don't retrieve a shoe, a stick or a dog toy. They just don't do the fetch thing. Nor the catch thing.

Throw a soft rubber ball for them to run after and you'll get a look that says, "you want me to do what?" Under their dog breath I'll hear a mumbled doggy version of: "Pendejo! you threw it, you go get it!" Tennis balls, bouncy balls or softballs do not excite the girls.

Toss a stick up ahead as you're walking, it will go completely ignored. Fling a Frisbee and it will become part of the landscape. Throw a ball, nothing. Kick a rock, not even a nod. There is no chase, no pursuit, no game. Boot a can, nothing, not a look, a twitch of the ear, or a lift of the brow. The girls could care less.

Labs, Retrievers, Setters, all love the game of fetch and catch. Tirelessly. Endlessly.

Dolce and Amore – NOT! Not even close! Not ever.

What they will run after is another pooch sprinting after the thrown object. Throw some balls and immediately the other visiting mutts will run over to play. Throw a stick, and Amore and Dolce will run after the other dog chasing after the stick. The game is all about chasing the other canines, not racing after the ball.

We'll take the girls to our dog park and lob some tennis balls their way. They'll sit at our feet watching us, their heads cocked at an angle, inquiring with a puzzled look, "wha'cha doing?" As soon as another dog moseys over for some fun, the girls perk up, ready to chase some tail which is much more fun than chasing a ball! What is the joy of running after a ball when you can race after another dog!

They will, however, chase after food. Chuck an apple twenty yards and Dolce is on it. Pitch some broccoli out in the field and it's a race to grab it first. Drop a bread crumb and it doesn't even hit the floor, gobbled and gone before you can bend down to pick it up.

However, there is one ball they will pursue. The one and only ball they will fetch and catch is a meatball! Lob, toss, fling, throw or drop a tasty, rolled meatball, cooked or raw, and it's caught mid-air in one gulp, down the hatch and in the gullet.

Eyes alert and on the "ball," they are ready for the next toss. Ready to catch it! Ready to race after it! Ready to eat it! Any kind of meatball, any kind of meat.

It's the only fetch and catch they'll play.

MUD

Dog doors are a great invention and our dog door was one of the better remodeling decisions Malcolm and I made.

When Tiamo was still a puppy, we added a large coyote-fenced enclosure that wrapped around the back of our New Mexican styled home. Aesthetically pleasing for the neighborhood, it fit in with the landscape. We deemed it the perfect dog pen.

We carefully planned the dog pen. The size, the gate placement, the amount of shade provided by the pinon trees. All were deliberately staged around Tiamo's needs. This was going to be her outside home for when we couldn't take her with us in the car and we wanted her comfortable. Nothing but the best for our Tiamo.

The one thing we didn't plan, was installing a dog door for an entrance to and fro from the pen into the house. Mistake number one. We didn't mind bringing her around the back to the outside pen entrance.

Tiamo's new playground was over 1,000 square feet of soft sand and shade. There were two large Pinon trees in the middle of the enclosure, providing protective cover from the sun. Plenty of room for her to run around. Plenty of room for her to play. Made and designed just for her, we were excited to introduce Tiamo to her new home away from home while at home.

Tiamo stepped one paw in the pen and hated it! She hated being left alone outside. She hated being separated from us. Most of all she hated knowing Thugs, our cat at the time, was indoors while she was suffering outdoors. She wanted to be with her humans.

She would dig deep holes under the gate, tunneling her way out to freedom, magically appearing at our back door. She scratched, clawed and budged her way out through any opening she could create. She would bend the gate frame, ripping the wiring.

We added reinforcements, new gate latches, heavier gauged wire, and still Tiamo would find a way out. One week after we christened our new dog pen addition, we abandoned it. Tiamo happily traded the pen for all the comforts of pillows and couches found inside our home.

For two years Tiamo's dog pen sat empty – until the puppies were born. The pen was the perfect dog park for eight little pups eager to explore and discover their new life. We would bring the kids out to the pen during the late hours of the afternoon, when the sun's heat was less severe. The entire litter would romp and play, sniff and scratch throughout the pen.

Tiamo, with her puppies, finally accepted the pen. In the fresh air, she tenderly watched over her rambunctious brood. The little ones rolled and tumbled for hours until we brought them back in to their make-shift pen set up in the garage. Tired and exhausted, the puppies would settle in a fast sleep for the night.

As each puppy left for their new life with their new human caregivers, Malcolm and I came to the conclusion we needed to add a dog door from the house to the pen for our remaining three;

Tiamo, Dolce and Amore. We needed an entrance from inside the house to the outside pen.

However, our careful planning of the pen's placement several years past failed to consider a common wall for a dog door. Mistake number two. We decided to install the dog door in our master bathroom's linen closet.

Malcolm and I patted ourselves on the back as we congratulated our egos with this smart plan. It was the perfect solution to adding a dog door. A bit unorthodox perhaps, placing the large unsightly door in our master bathroom, but very practical to our way of thinking. We could hide the flap easily, close the door off if needed, and at the same time, have a door for access to the pen. It was the perfect solution.

Installation day was on a Friday, the first of July. We wanted to have the door installed and finished before our Monsoon Season started so the girls could come inside, out of the rain.

Training our three girls to use the dog door was simple and easy. A tasty nugget of ground hamburger was all it took to entice Tiamo through the small opening, with Amore and Dolce quickly following. A meatball on the flip side brought Tiamo back through the opening. It wasn't long before each dog was barreling through the flap looking for a nibble of ground beef.

The girls immediately used the outdoors as they should, doing their duty discreetly outside. No more getting up to let one of the dogs out, no more waiting in the freezing cold as Dolce sniffed for the perfect spot, no more chasing after Amore as she sensed freedom. Life was just made easier, all due to a dog door. A rubber flap. Life was great! Malcolm and I both sighed in relief.

Five days after the installation, our monsoon rains came. Blessed drops of liquid fell onto our parched acreage. Never lasting very long, the afternoon showers can alternate from a gentle pitter-patter to hard torrents of destruction. The dry land will soak up the falling moisture like a sponge, filling its cracks with water, letting the excess flow over into arroyos creating flash floods.

Not only do our summer storms bequeath us with fiery sunsets that paint the sky with vibrant colors, they also leave us with clay dirt that quickly becomes both thick and slick. It clings to our shoes, dragging your footsteps with the extra weight of the mud.

It was on a day such as this, that I came home from work to discover mud, lots of mud, strewn from one end of the house to the other! There were muddy paws prints in every room, every part of the house. On the sofa, on the bed, everywhere. Oh. My. God. What had happened? I was in total shock.

The girls came running to greet me, each with a wet, muddy underbelly, each filthy and dirty, mud and sludge oozing from what was once their white paws. And each with a huge happy grin on their face. It wasn't long before all their mud became my mud. With each dog greeting me, I quickly had mud all over me.

Our new dog door was a gateway to mud and muck. Mistake number three!

Luckily, we have brick floors. And, we have a great house cleaner, who loves our dogs.

CHI CHI WOW WOW!

Rug rats. Carpet crawlers. Couch climbers. Those tiny little two-legged adorable tots known to mankind as kids.

In our case, kids that belong to someone else. Malcolm and I don't have children, we have dogs. At one time we had three large, very demanding Bernese Mountain Dogs. Now two. Still just as demanding. Though they might look mature, and they might be well pass the terrible twos phase, they still act like KIDS!

And, like kids, they can be expensive. No, we don't worry about paying for braces, prom or college. We worry about the price of dog food. We worry about vet bills, boarding costs and we worry about bath time.

There is nothing a small toddler enjoys more than to run screaming through the house after bath time. A bare bottom streaking by as their parents chase after them with a dry towel, trying to catch the slippery little munchkin.

As my mother would say, "Chi chi wow wow!!" exclamation mark, exclamation mark, producing giggles and laughs from the two-year old flasher a.k.a. her grandkid.

Our girls pretty much do the same thing. Run. Away. Bath time brings out all sorts of bad behavior and antics as Dolce and Amore attempt to avoid the soap and water.

When Dolce and Amore were little puppies, we could give them a bath ourselves, usually in the kitchen sink. Still small enough, we would put their front paws in one side of the double-sink, the back paws over the divider and into the other side. Using the handy-dandy faucet nozzle to wet them, soap them and rinse, they struggled to stop the process.

I can tell ya', they didn't enjoy their baths. One of us always needed to keep a tight hold on them while the other washed, as they squirmed and wiggled, trying to find their way to freedom. As we scrubbed them, there was more soap and water on us than in the sink.

Just like a little tyke, the minute we set them down from the high counters after their rub down, they would streak through the house. Usually trying for the pen, where they could roll in the dirt, undoing all our work.

Eventually Malcolm and I wised up, blocking the entrance to the outside pen. Dolce and Amore retaliated by jumping up on the living room couch, rolling their still wet bodies over the cushions and pillows, leaving wet dog hair and fur in their wake. UCK! Plus more clean up. It has been a battle ever since.

When the girls grew too big for the sink, they graduated to the double-headed shower in our master bath. A shower large enough for both Malcolm and I, swimsuit clad, to bathe them. One holding, one scrubbing. That lasted two tries. Amore learned to tolerate the water and the cleansing. Dolce absolutely hated it.

There is no blocking a determined dog. When Dolce has had enough and wants out of the shower, she's gone. Dog-gone gone. The first sniff of freedom and she is shaking the water. All over the bathroom. Soap and water drops scattering up to the 14 ft.

ceiling and sideways, landing on mirrors, counters, and cabinets. There isn't a dry spot available. She is rolling on her back, leaving locks of her fur on the floor mats, the bricks and every other surface.

There is one phase of grooming Dolce does love and that is the rub down. With lots of towels. I mean a lot of towels. Which means a lot of washing afterwards.

To be honest, Malcolm and I didn't like it much ourselves. Bathing the dogs killed our backs, being bent over as we scrubbed. Wet dog fur adhered all over us in big clumps. The shower clean up took just as long as the actual dog grooming. No, we didn't like bathing our fully grown girls one bit.

After two attempts to bathe Dolce and Amore ourselves, we gave up. Time for the groomers. Well, that was a mistake.

Not only is it horribly expensive for a large dog, however justified it is, at the time, we had three Berners. Triple the cost. The total grooming bill for three before tax and tip was around $300 big ones. Triple Net. With more to add to the bill, we decided we needed an alternative.

Tiamo was used to going to the dog groomers. Didn't like it, put on the front paw brakes when we entered the establishment, but she endured the process. And when we were paying for just one dog, the expense wasn't as hard to swallow. Add Dolce and Amore to the invoice and we would be eating rice and beans for the month.

Enter Tara, our puppy-sitting college student friend. Silly her! Tara raised her hand the highest to volunteer to bathe our dogs. But what college student doesn't want a bit of beer money?

Tara was our life-saver. We named the date, purchased the necessary supplies for washing, grabbed all our towels for rub downs and pointed her to our huge shower. Done!

Our shrieks of "get back in here" to a dog racing out of the shower, that: A) does not listen; and, B) is absolutely meaningless to a 100 pound wet dog determined to avoid a bath, has quieted.

Malcolm and I now coo, "Chi Chi Wow Wow!!" as Dolce and Amore parade past us sweet-smelling, with fluffy clean fur. All due to Tara!

Yeeeee haaaaw!

MISSING MOM & DAD

June is one of those transition months for the dogs. The days are longer, hotter, and walks for the dogs are delayed to the evening hours, when it starts to cool down. More often than not, Dolce and Amore are left at home, not wanting to leave them in the car during the hot hours of the day as Malcolm or I run into town for errands.

Malcolm and I are busier. Between work, travel, meetings, weddings, graduations and Saturday night dinners – it seems we're gone more than we're home. The girls feel the effect of our busy schedule and don't necessarily like it. Not one bit.

Flanked between boredom, and long hot days, they alternate between being sluggish during the hottest parts of the day to being antsy when the tedious hours of lonesomeness labors on. They don't quite understand why their daily schedule has shifted to accommodate June's higher temperatures and our demanding agendas.

It's the aftershock effects of dog boredom that Malcolm and I try to eliminate. We try not to be gone for much more that a few hours at a stretch. We try to ensure Dolce and Amore have been fed prior to our leaving. We try to schedule a walk in the hours before we take off, hoping to leave them tired and ready for a doggy nap while we are absent. We try anything and everything that will keep them from destroying the household in the few hours we are away.

Destroy, wreck, obliterate, are mild descriptions of the havoc Dolce and Amore might create and cause. Words like annihilate, demolish and raze really don't do justice to their imaginative destruction. As we have learned, there is truth to the saying "when the cat's away, the mice will play."

We have returned home to chewed up library books, all with a pricy fines attached to them when we return the dog-tagged books. Important papers and magazines left on an end table quickly become fodder for mastication entertainment. Every once in a while I get to go shoe shopping. Not that I mind I mean, come on, it's shoe shopping, but it does get expensive replacing the same black pumps. It hurts our pocketbook each and every time their creative destructiveness is activated.

We have discovered scratched plaster and paint from under our high kitchen counter walls, expanding to an even larger destroyed surface area the next time we were gone. Before we have a chance to re-plaster and paint the exposed area, the girls have managed to poke a huge hole through the drywall into the cabinet on the other side. Turned out that there was a nice little mouse nest in the unused cabinet. The dogs weren't destructive monsters, they just wanted the mouse.

Doors have been scratched, articles of clothing dragged out to the pen, plates have been broken as the girls counter-surfed their way through boredom.

Rugs have been heaved hoed and hauled into other rooms, due to Dolce and Amore's bouts of sumo wrestling in the hallways. In other times, the rugs are tugged through the dog door just because we aren't home to stop it. Just because they can. It's become routine to perform a "pen check" on our return from being gone.

All the mayhem, all the demolition, all because mom and dad aren't home. It makes the welcome home party all the more exciting. Malcolm and I never know what to expect when we enter from being away.

Once the girls hear the car tires crunching the gravel as we coast down the driveway, when they hear the garage door roll up on its tracks, they go ballistic. Their enthusiasm knowing mom and dad are back home is beyond happy. Beyond exhilaration.

Simply put, Dolce and Amore want to be with us. Constantly. Always. When they are separated from us, they don't like it. When we are away from them, they don't like it. When they are left at home, they don't like it.

The initial canine meet and greet at the door is a wild frenzy of jumping dogs and excited barking. It's a whirlwind of trying to get through the door and being welcomed home. It's a rush of paws, fur and slobbering dogs, both of which want their share of love and attention.

I know we shouldn't encourage a hundred pound jumping dog, or the excited greeting of indoor, loud barking. However, the special hug I receive from Dolce when she places her front paws on my hips and gives me a squeeze, or when Amore moves besides her to join in the kum-ba-yah moment isn't something I ever want to stop.

We can easily spend forty or so minutes calming them down as we enter the house after being away. Both Dolce and Amore get clingy, wanting us right by them, touching us with their paws, nose nudging our hands and elbows. They just want our touch. A hand resting on them. A constant scratch under the chin. Fingers endlessly rubbing their fur-lined ears. A belly scratch.

The usual scenario is a furry body on each side of me on the couch, so close a sheet of paper couldn't slide between us, my arms around each one. If I so much as move a finger away or twitch an eyelid, they'll nudge me with their powerful paws as a reminder to pay more attention to them. Their hind ends burrow in even deeper into the corner pocket between the couch and my hip, their bodies leaning into me. I have 100 lbs. of deadweight dog resting against me on each side. And, I love it. All of it.

They each have their spot – Dolce on my left, tucked in close under my arm and shoulder, eyes closed in satisfaction. Amore on my right, plastered to my side, head resting against me, an occasional lick to my hand. I'm somewhere in the middle breathing in dog hair and fending off paws and noses.

They missed us. They missed mom and dad. It's a wonderful testament of a dog's love for its caregivers.

THE BLACK HOLE

A sock goes missing. Pens disappear. Car keys that were just in your hand are gone. Eyeglasses lost. The creamer that you placed on the kitchen counter after pouring yourself some coffee, vanished. Your cell phone misplaced.

The next scene shows you scratching your head as you wander around your house looking for the no-where-to-be-found items. Geez! You just had 'em, where could they be?

You're not senile, you're not losing your mind, it's not loss of memory, but damn, where could they be?

In my case, it was my cell phone.

At 6:30 a.m.

On a work day.

I checked my car, under the seats, between the console looking for my missing phone. I re-checked my purse and all its pockets that have been my designated personal filing cabinet for years – no luck.

I'm not crazy! I just placed my whole connection to my life, my friends, my business associates on the kitchen table and now it's gone. AWOL. At first I was puzzled. What did I do with my phone? I just had it.

I retraced my steps, back tracked in my mind the rooms I had just been in. I checked the coat I were wearing last, under pillows, behind cushions. Nowhere. Gone. Missing.

I patted down my back pants pockets, my front pockets, my chest pockets, the proverbial phone shelf and came up empty. I grabbed my husband's phone and dialed my number only to hear nothing. I forgot that I had shut it off the day before for a meeting. My photo album, my phone book, my email list – gone, gone, gone. Now I was getting anxious. Where was my phone?

Amore was picking up on my anxious state, following me as I went from room to room hunting down my cell. Dolce was nowhere to be found.

I have to admit, especially since I am talking a lost phone, I went from puzzled to anxious to frantic in about 60 seconds flat. The sounds from my heels tapping against the brick floor started clicking faster and faster in my desperation to locate my cell. I was in frantic mode and Amore was right along with me. Amore was stirred up.

Dogs seem to pick up on their human folk's emotional state and Amore had zeroed in on mine. She started to run through the house barking her way from one end to the other. Her loud barks were a beacon for Dolce, calling her in from the outside.

It's standard procedure between the two of them, if one dog barks, the other will join in the chorus singing back-up. The duet woke up Malcolm. Crap!

"What the hell is going on?" a blurry eyed Malcolm growled.

"Can't find my cell phone," I tersely replied. I was frustrated.

"Try the pen. Dolce has been frantically coming in and out of the pen for the last 15 minutes, making a racket with the dog flap," he mumbled as he rolled back over in bed, pulling the covers up and over his head. He didn't want any more noise, barking or heel clacking.

I trooped around the back to the dog pen, Amore and Dolce running through the house to meet up with me in the back. They were just coming through the dog flap as I was opening the heavy gate. Yep. There lay my cell phone, under a dog-torn bush. Thankfully unharmed, unscathed. A little drool on the back side. It seemed Dolce was the culprit. The phone perpetrator. Our thief.

There was the beginnings of a hole being dug to the left of my phone. Fresh dirt nosed into a small pile, leading me to believe that Dolce was going to bury the evidence. Her prize, my phone. That might have been a first, a dog buried cell phone. Her muzzle still had a sprinkle of dirt around the nose.

I wasn't in the mood to laugh about it. I snatched up my phone, wiped off the remaining dirt and drool and hi-tailed it to work.

Later, after my committee meeting, after I was home from work, after my sense of humor kicked back in, I could (and would) chuckle over Dolce and the black hole.

Later, Malcolm and I would have a hoot over what else might be buried in the dog pen, laughing about what else might be missing.

But not now!

Now, when something is missing, the pen is the first place we look.

SNEAKY SNAKE

We have a sneaky snake. No, it's not Dolce, who is usually our first choice to blame. She likes to double-back on the trail to sneak a bite at a road apple or two. Nor is it Amore, a likely culprit, who likes to quietly slip into the kitchen undetected to counter-surf for any and all crumbs left behind.

Both girls have well-deserved and well-earned reputations of being sly, cunning, evasive, clever, crafty… and, well, just down-right sneaky when it comes to a delicious little tidbit of food that they desire.

They are pros when it comes to measuring the distance between their human masters (us), the goal (food), and the trials and tribulations that lay in and between the said goal. They can recognize the challenge and can process the steps necessary to achieve food-stealing victory without being scared or turning back. And, usually they are spot-on thieves, quick as a wink and unafraid of retribution from Malcolm or myself.

No, this sneaky snake is just that, a snake. A real one. Four to five feet long, I can only pray it is either a Bull Snake, Whip Snake, or a Red Racer. Of course, by the time I finish this epic tale, the snake will be at least six to seven feet long with a girth wider than Malcolm's chest and has fangs to rival a vampire dripping with blood.

Unfortunately, the only evidence we have gathered so far is the found shed skin. A long, scaly, ugly paper-thin snake-skin.

Uck! Double uck! Triple, quadruple, uck! Let me say it in plain English - UCK! UCK! UCK!

I. HATE. SNAKES!!!!!! How many exclamation marks do you need here?

Big, small, skinny, fat, friendly or deadly, doesn't matter, I hate 'em all and it doesn't help matters that I live in an area that is populated with such serpents. Give me a spider or a mouse any day.

I know, without a doubt, if Dolce or Amore ever saw a snake they would think it's play time, something to chase after, play with and perhaps bring into the house to show off to the folks. Amore loves lizards; a snake would just be an extension of her lizard play.

When Tiamo was around six months old, she did just that. She had found a small baby snake about 8 inches long and promptly brought it into the house to show off her find. I screamed!

Clutched within her jaw, dangling out both sides of her mouth, Tiamo was proud of her snake catch. I screamed again! And then jumped to the highest table away from the ugly reptile.

"MALCOLM!" the third scream had him running into the kitchen. Notice it took three screams?

"What the hell?" he was bewildered as he came to a stop from sprinting in from outside. He saw me on the kitchen table, screaming and pointing to Tiamo. All he saw was Tiamo with a short, dark string in her mouth. Then he looked closer.

"It's a SNAKE!" I was shaking. Did I mention I hate snakes? "Get it away from her!" I ordered. He did. Somehow. Tiamo didn't want to give up her prize. She was showing off her catch.

I have no idea what type of snake it might have been. Hopefully not a Rattlesnake. It was too small to tell. I'm only thankful it was already dead when she found it. Dead snakes I can almost, barely, just maybe, handle. Wiggly snakes and still alive snakes, there is no way in hell.

With the frequent monsoon rains we receive during the summer months, many rodents and reptiles move up to higher ground. We easily see more snakes, mice, pack rats, moles, voles and gophers in one day following a rain, than we will all year long.

To date, in all the years we've lived in New Mexico, the total varmint and reptile count we have seen is: 12 Rattlesnakes, 4 Bull Snakes, 2 Whip Snakes and 6 Red Racers – a zillion Kangaroo Rats, a couple hundred Pack Rats (imagine a mouse on steroids) and at least 12 gophers. Mice and lizards aren't part of the totals, as they are beyond counting. The bottom line: that is twenty-four snakes too many!

Every spring we give Tiamo, Dolce and Amore a Rattlesnake booster shot. We are vigilant when we hike the trails and the nearby green belt. Miles from anywhere with no cell service, we are always looking out for the slimy things. And, even though it's often said, "they are more afraid of you" – I still fret and worry about snakes.

When the winter weather turns into spring, warming up the landscape, I start to worry about snakes. I start warning Malcolm to keep a sharp eye out for them on the trail when he walks the girls. I am constantly preaching to Malcolm he needs to be alert.

"Be snake smart," I advise him. Okay, I most likely nag him to death and I know he ignores me most of the time. Until one day after he came back from walking the dogs.

"Guess what I saw today?" he asked.

"What?" I asked back, "

"A Rattlesnake. Dolce and Amore walked right past it. Didn't even see it," Malcolm replied. My fear of what the girls would do when confronted by a snake escalated.

"What did you do?" I questioned him.

"I got the hell out of dodge!"

"Was it very big? How far away was it? Did it see you?" I didn't let up on the interrogation. In other words, were you in striking distance? I wanted all the details.

Malcolm stretched out his arms, "it was about this big," he replied. "And, maybe from here to the couch away." I calculated the distance to be about ten feet. Safe enough. Rattlesnakes can strike within two-thirds or so of their full length, give or take an inch. A five to six foot snake in length can attack from within approximately three to four feet of its striking zone. Even so, when it comes to snakes, ten feet is ten feet too close.

Once, mid-to-late-summer, I came from around the back corner of our house only to find Gordita on the ledge of our back portal, sitting on her haunches on the bricks, peering over the edge.

As I came a little closer, I saw a five-foot snake stretched out along the garden bed directly below our bricked portal. Gordita calmly eyeing the thing. The snake not moving. Gordita was intently watching the snake.

"Ah, hell! Now we have a snake hanging out near our home!" My second thought was it looked like a Rattlesnake. Of course, everything looks like a Rattlesnake to me. Upon closer inspection, both Malcolm and I realized it was a Bull snake.

Bull snakes, at first glance, do look similar to a Rattlesnake. They are non-poisonous but can be aggressive, coiling into a striking position when threatened, resembling a Rattlesnake.

The only good thing about any kind of snake is they keep the rodent population down to a minimum. However, if I have to have a snake living close to the house, I'm glad it's a Bull snake.

"Do something!" I demanded of my Eagle Scout husband.

"What do you want me to do? It's a snake and it's outside. Leave it alone," Malcolm reasoned.

My husband. My Great Protector.

THE BOWLS

There are two kinds of bowls in our house - the animal water bowl and the toilet bowl. They both provide an endless supply of hydration for our dogs and Gordita.

Each dog has a preference. Each has a favored style of water distribution and each has a unique way of sipping their fluids. Gordita just drinks whatever is convenient, mainly from the water bowl. I think she is too fat to try the toilet bowl. That would require too much energy to jump up on the seat.

Dolce fancies running water, preferably from a hose. She'll crouch down, tip her head under the nozzle and "bite" the flowing water.

For the longest time, Dolce had the misfortune of having to use a standard dog water bowl, hoses not being the norm for the inside of our house. I am now thinking she did so under duress.

On hikes, she'll only drink from the bottle as we're pouring the water into the fold-up canvas trail bowl, never from the nylon lined cavity. Out in the pen, she'll ignore the water bowls and the rain puddles and instead lap up the tiny drops of moisture emitting from the drip irrigation line stationed around the Pinon trees. In the back yard, she prays for the hose to be turned on. Dolce has even learned to wait a few seconds until the warm hose water left in the line turns to cold.

Beside me as I'm tinkering about in the yard, Dolce will eagerly wait for me to turn on the hose, anticipating immediate flowing water. I chuckle over the puzzled look of confusion she gives me, as she waits for the water to run through the 150 ft. of hose, until the water shoots out the nozzle directly in her open jaws, turning her confusion into surprise. It has turned into a game with her, as she waits for that first shot of water to hit her, timing her mouth to open at just the right moment. She loves it!

And, then one day Uncle Dan came to visit.

Dan is a long-time friend of Malcolm's and adores the girls. He always brings the girls a special treat when he comes to visit. Toys, smoked bones, treats, he spoils 'em rotten. Dan is one of our many guests that get invited back. Not only cuz he's been a friend of Malcolm's for over 40 years, but because he loves our girls.

On his last visit, he shipped out the BigDog Bowl. A dog-watering contraption with constant running water being pumped through. I, of course, love anyone who loves our girls, so Dan can do no wrong!

Dan arrived on a Wednesday and the following day the BigDog Bowl arrived. Malcolm and Dan immediately performed the set-up. The Bowl came with so many parts I think they had to actually read the instructions on how to assemble the bowl. Within an hour or so, the bowl was ready for use.

The minute Dolce heard the running water she ran over to investigate. She quickly realized she had running water indoors and immediately claimed the bowl as hers. It took her all of 20 seconds for her to tip her head down and start biting the water. She likes to stand to the right side of the bowl, crouch down and beeline into the fountain. Dolce was in heaven! Indoor running water. Uncle Dan just became our #1 guest. All because of the BigDog Bowl.

Amore on the other hand, prefers the toilet. It's just the right height, just the right temperature of coldness, just the right size for water delivery. She likes the master bath's porcelain the best, as it is closest to the dog pen and her dog pillow. The guest bathroom's throne is used only if it's a "have-to" situation.

She'll stand at the bowl for a good four to five minutes, slurping and lapping the cool water, sometimes draining the basin.

Amore will drink some, think a little, drink some more, think a little more, and then maybe drink some more again. She'll take her time, stare off in space for a few seconds, then dip her head back down to the bowl for a few more sips. There is a method, a process to drinking water.

She'll then leave a 15 ft. trail of huge water drops into the bedroom and through the house. Thank gawd for brick floors!

Malcolm grumbles about cleaning the BigDog bowl. It comes with a lot of parts and pieces and cleaning has become a weekly chore. His chore. He grumbles, but he cleans it because he knows Dolce loves running water and he wants fresh water for her. He grumbles about receiving a gift that takes so much work. He grumbles about how dirty the water gets and how fast. He grumbles about it and yet he takes such joy in seeing Dolce bite at the water.

We've yet to see Amore drink from the BigDog bowl, not even from the wide bottom basin holding the overflow. We haven't figured out if it is the noise of the trickling water, the ripple effect in the lower basin or if she just doesn't like lowering her muzzle to sip some water.

Bottom line – she refuses to drink from the BigDog bowl.

Now Malcolm goes around the house flushing clean toilets, just to refill her bowl and release some "fresh" water. I leave a towel close by to "wipe-the-drips" on the seat for later.

How spoiled is that?

☁ THUNDER

For several years running, New Mexico has been in a terrible drought. With water rationing and conservation signage throughout our restaurants and hotels, New Mexicans have learned to sip and dip carefully. Every winter, we pray for snow and rain. Every summer we pray for a heavy-handed monsoon season.

Some summers, we are lucky. Deluged with a plentiful and steady monsoon season, the rains will bring buckets of precious water to our parched landscape, leaving knee-high weeds mingling within a plethora of wildflowers. We then see our high desert countryside so green, so lush with foliage, so full of nature. It's beautiful. With each rain, the elevated fire danger alerts lessen. The fire gauge's arrow slowly creeping back from red to orange to yellow to green.

Other times, early in the summer, we might see fires in the Jemez Mountains to our west or fires in the Pecos Wilderness to our east. Usually started by lightening. Sometimes arson. Our mornings will bring a smoky haze creeping around Santa Fe, our afternoons will show us billowing smoke clouds topping the Sangre de Cristos.

We hold our breath each time we hear thunder, fearing a lightning strike against the nature caused dryness. When the monsoons arrive in July, our tension eases, knowing the pinon trees and grasses will be soaking up the moisture, re-building their arsenal against the ever-present dryness.

Some time around the first part of July, we usually receive our first round of monsoon showers. The rains help lower the day's high temperature and add moisture for our plants and foliage. The normal thunder and lightning come along for the ride.

I can remember one summer when we first had Tiamo, we were awakened at 2:00 a.m. in the morning with a loud crash, jolting us out of bed. A summer storm was directly overhead and was flashing its tail in all its glory. The lightening was so close you could read by the light of it. It was a beautiful sight. The thunder crashing around us like cymbals in a parade. It lasted for a good thirty minutes before the storm slowly moved on. Tiamo slept right through it. Didn't faze her in the least.

Malcolm and I were relieved when Dolce and Amore seemed okay with our summer storms. Neither were bothered by the pounding thunder or the lightening cracks whipping across the sky. Most of the time, they didn't even lift their heads off their pillows when the rolling thunder reverberated through the air. They took the force of nature in stride. We were fortunate the vociferous clashing noise didn't worry them. All three dogs didn't seem to mind the storms.

Until, out of the clear blue, Amore decided she did not like thunder. In fact, she decided she was downright scared of thunder. So scared, and so unexpected, the first time she freaked, we immediately took her to the vet, knowing something was horribly wrong. Amore had never been afraid of our monsoons. Ever. She had never been fearful of thunder. Ever. She was five years old and had never indicated she had issues with thunder or lightening. Ever.

Shivering, shaking, not eating, agitated, up and down, insistent to be on us or right next to us, we were clueless to what was wrong with her. Amore was terrified. Two hundred dollars later, our vet had no idea what was wrong with Amore either.

We purchased a thunder shirt for her, hoping to lessen her anxiety. The moment we heard the distant rumbling drums of thunder, we put Amore in her shirt, wrapping the fabric snugly against her. It helped. Not completely, but it brought her panic to a more manageable level. Her shaking was minimalized. Her shivers more subdued.

Three storms later, Amore associated the thunder shirt with thunder. When she saw us gather the shirt to wrap it around her, she knew the booming noise was returning. Coming fast on the heels of her wearing the shirt, her shaking would start up. We were back in the same boat, with Amore just as scared and frightened as before.

For five years, thunder's loud roll overhead never affected Amore. Today, even distant reverberations bring her to her knees. Whimpering, shaking, scared.

Most summer rains in New Mexico bring rounds of thunder. Usually late in the afternoon and at night. Once, at one in the morning, Amore awoke in fear as the storm let loose above us. Lightning, thunder, rain, and hail crashed around us throughout the night, pelting the land with more than an inch of moisture in less than forty minutes.

Amore shook with terror as the loud booms of thunder were clashing over us. She headed straight to Malcolm to calm her, jumping up on the bed and onto Malcolm's sleeping form.

"Oomph!" the air pushed out of Malcolm's lungs as Amore landed on him.

"What the HELL!" I heard from the other side of the bed. Malcolm was confronted by a panicked Amore.

Malcolm woke to a trembling dog crushing him, breathing in dog hair, a dog tail flapping in his face. Paws stepping all over him, forget the thunder shirt, Malcolm was Amore's security blanket. She wanted only Malcolm.

It was sunrise before Malcolm was able to calm Amore down, and fall back to sleep. When I woke, Amore was nestled up against his side, gently snoring.

Safe.

S.N.O.U.T WRESTLING

The dogs love it when company arrives. It's even better if the visitors are over-night guests. Dolce and Amore understand the more humans there are in the house, the more people there are to give them some love and attention. Lots of attention.

A long weekend visit from guests is nirvana to them. They know additional people hanging out equals more lovin' and more lovin' equals more petting and belly rubs. Lots of belly rubs. Yes sirree bob, the girls do love our company.

To Dolce and Amore, house guests equates to another unsuspecting victim foolish enough to place their "petting hand" at nose height. Just low enough to finagle a head rub from the gullible guest, or a scratch to the ear, or if they're really lucky, a full body massage. Yep, Dolce and Amore have it all figured out.

I tell ya', we have smart dogs, and they know their math. Multiplied by the number of guests, Dolce and Amore can calculate the amount of adoration they should be receiving, and for how long. They have both learned to work it!

An empty hand to the side is all the inspiration they need to give the same hand a little nose nudge, a little encouragement for a scratch, a caress, a rub.

A second gentle nose nudge to the hand, serving as a courtesy reminder, is quickly given when a houseguest isn't paying enough attention to their rubbings, when the petting starts to be a bit absentminded, or when the caressing slows to a stop.

This soft nose nudge is usually good for another seven or so minutes of full attention. Additional nudges can easily add another two to three minutes on to their massage session. By the fifth nudge, the girls are under duress.

Fifth and sixth nose nudges are delivered only when the petting hand has completely stopped all contact. It no longer qualifies as a nose nudge – Dolce and Amore are now into a full on, no-holds-barred, S.N.O.U.T. Wrestling approach.

S.N.O.U.T. Wrestling occurs about 24-36 hours after the guests arrive, just about the time when the novelty of the dogs has worn off. The moment when our guests are tired of petting and rubbing. It usually starts with Amore, eager for more lovin' and attention, illegally using her muzzle to gain your attention.

It almost always ends with a foul being called: Unnecessary Roughness. Offense. Ten yard penalty. Normally after a drink has been tossed into the air, only to land back on a clean shirt, after a distraught hooch hooter has jolted your arm upright. That, my friends, is S.N.O.U.T. Wrestling at it's best.

Coined by Ken, one our favorite guests, S.N.O.U.T. Wrestling stands for STRONG NOSE ON ULNA & TIBIA. For Dolce and Amore, it means business.

At best, S.N.O.U.T. Wrestling might give the dogs a few extra minutes of rubbing. Usually, it just encourages our guests to move to higher ground – a tall bar stool, out of reach from Dolce's strong nose. Or better yet, in a standing position with the tall stool arranged as a barricade from Amore's attempt to mutt muzzle her way for more consideration, more ear scratching, more rubbing.

At it's worst, S.N.O.U.T. Wrestling will bring irritated shouts of "NO!," "STOP IT!," and/or "QUIT!," sometimes all three and hopefully without someone tripping or falling after losing their balance from a brief S.N.O.U.T. wrestle. It almost always results in a spilled beverage and some soiled clothes.

S.N.O.U.T. Wrestling begins with their muzzle, usually under your arm, sometimes behind your leg. Lifting at a high rate of force, thrust, and energy, it can be powerful.

There is enough torque behind their lift to fling your arm up so fast if you were a Barbie doll your plastic arm would twist off. The lift dominance is so substantial that visits to the E.R. are a possibility. Malcolm and I have been extremely fortunate there haven't been any medical emergencies caused by S.N.O.U.T. Wrestling.

The move is always unexpected, even when you're expecting it. It is always quick, with no notice, and gets the pin - shoulders on the mat!

Our unsuspecting house guests are often lured into believing one of the two dogs has given up and moved on. NOT! Not on your life! They have only moved into position, behind the gullible guest, out of visibility, staying under radar. Placing their muzzle at a forty-five degree angle, shoulders dipped slightly for spring, they lay in wait for the elbow to lower at just the right height.

Bam!

You've been S.N.O.U.T.ed. By a con-artist. By a pro. Just like that! Dolce and Amore are both experts at S.N.O.U.T. Wrestling. Pros at it. Probably the best in the business. I've yet to see another dog as successful at S.N.O.U.T. Wrestling than Dolce or Amore.

Whatever you were holding in your hand has flown into the air in route to another household galaxy. Orbited into space like a meteor heading towards earth, there will be shattering consequences arriving in three or less seconds.

Insistent, intrusive and annoying, S.N.O.U.T. Wrestling is the dogs at their brattiest and way past the point of cute, but, on the flip side, it keeps the company from staying too long!

CLEAN SHEETS

Fall is always a busy time for me. The just-starting-to-turn-nippy months found on the back end of the calendar are penciled in with conferences, meetings and annual conventions. All requiring travel. All requiring me to be gone.

Late September, early October, I usually attend a national Conference for the Council of MLS. They rotate the location of the convention around the states, alternating between the East coast and the Western states. One year the conference was held in Boise, Idaho – land of the potato and the famous blue field.

A State enriched in western history and culture, Idahoans have earned the right to boast about their beautiful state. From the Snake River that weaves its way throughout Idaho, leaving rich, fertile farm lands in its wake, to the mountainous peaks in the pan-handle, Idaho is an enchanting parcel of land.

Away for a full week, it goes without saying that I missed my husband and our dogs while I was gone. A lot. A lot, a lot. A lot, a lot, a lot!

But not on the first day away. Not at all. Not one second. The first day was a novelty, a rare occasion of being away from the girls.

Day one was reserved for enjoying the huge king-sized bed all to myself – no dogs pinning me under the covers, no dog hair adhered to the down pillows, no cat stretched out along side of my back, hotter than a furnace cranked on high in the middle of summer.

Nope. Day one was spent luxuriating between clean six hundred count Egyptian cotton sheets with my toes curling and flexing under the crisp freshness that comes with a four-diamond rated hotel. Day one was perfect.

It's pure bliss just to stretch out without being blocked by a dog. Pure heaven to have a minimum of four down pillows to pick from. Yep. On the first day, I didn't miss one single dog hair.

And, I didn't really miss 'back home' too much on days two and three and sort-of on day four.

These days were just extensions of the first day – being in Egyptian sheet heaven. I loved the down pillows. I loved the heavy crisp cotton sheets. I loved being able to watch T.V. while indulging in the vast bed I had to myself. Days two and three were nearly perfect.

Days two, three and half of four were working days. These were the days I kept busy with meetings, speakers and sessions, starting early and ending the day late. These were the days I was networking, meeting fellow association directors. I didn't even have a chance or the time to miss "back-home." And, no, I didn't miss one single dog hair.

On day two and three, I didn't smell like dog. I didn't have to wipe my hand on my pants legs before I shook hands with an acquaintance. And best of all, I had the king sized bed to myself. Oh yeah, you guys have no idea how great that is.

By day three I realized I hadn't once used the 'dog-hair-lint-roller' brush I always carry with me. I'd been dog-hair free for three whole fantastic days. My white sweaters were still white, my business dress pants were drool free. I didn't leave any stray dog hairs on the luncheon tablecloth.

By day four and a half, I discovered the bed really wasn't as great as it was cracked up to be. What was the fun of watching television if there was no one to fight with over the remote control? What good was a huge bed if the dogs were a thousand miles away? What good was any of it without my family? Day four was starting to be not so perfect. On day four I was missing "back home." I was starting to miss dog hair.

On day's five through seven, the scales tipped.

My six hundred count utopia was starting to loose its charm. The conference was over. Check out time had arrived and I was still in Boise. I had stayed some extra days to enjoy Idaho with some long-time friends, Alex and Celia, who summer in Boise. I was glad to visit with them, it was wonderful to see them, but I was starting to miss home. Missing Malcolm, missing my girls. I was missing dog hair!

And Gordita. I missed our fat cat. I missed having to pick her up so she could reach her food bowl because she is too heavy to jump herself. I missed her being curled up next to me on the couch. I missed her purring hum. I missed my kids and their stray hairs.

I was missing Malcolm, laughing over silly things, commenting on the day's events. I missed kissing him good morning, his welcoming hug in the evening. Day seven was hell. It was way past the time to be home.

I was missing my girls, their sweet love, their tender nudges, their crazy antics. I was missing the dogs on the bed – on their backs, paws in the air as they slept, gentle snores washing over them. I was missing their sound-asleep weight leaning against my legs, the cat up by my head. I was missing my family. I was missing dog hair.

I flew home on day eight.

I asked Malcolm to bring the dogs with him, when he came to pick me up at the airport. I embraced the thought of knowing I'd be covered in dog hair in a nano second once I climbed in the car. I knew I would have two dogs clamoring to hug me, paw me, and lick me once I had my seat belt buckled. I knew I would have Dolce sitting on my lap the second the seat belt clicked.

And I couldn't wait!

Crisp, fresh clean sheets were just a dim memory. The dog haired love waiting for me in the car far out-weighed and out-counted my six hundred thread count Egyptian Cotton sheets.

SNOW ANGELS

A tired dog is a happy owner! Yup, Malcolm and I live by that saying. We totally believe in it. And nothing tires out our girls more than snow.

The northern part of New Mexico is considered high desert. Depending on which little cactus infested hill your house perches on, you could easily be sitting at 7500 feet elevation. We definitely get snow. Not always very much, and it tends to melt away by mid-morning, but Santa Fe does receive its fair share of snow.

Once or twice a year, we'll wake up to an abundance of snow on the ground. Maybe three to six inches, with even higher levels from snow drifts. The snow comes in quietly throughout the night, softly falling on the juniper boughs and the cactus spines. It's not like rain where you hear it hitting the flat roof and the windows. It's quiet. Silent. Snow mornings are always a surprise.

When Santa Fe gets two to three inches it's a Snow Day. It's enough to shut down the City Different. Enough for the schools and government offices to close shop for a snow day. Enough for me to work from home, still in my robe. Enough for others from snow-laddened areas across the nation to laugh – they have no problem driving to work with eighteen inches of freshly fallen snow.

But even three inches of snow is enough for the girls to have some fun!

Play time in the snow is probably Dolce and Amore's number one favorite doings. In the life of our dogs, there is nothing better than a full belly, a warm bed and then a romp in the snow. They've never had it so good.

A week after one of our first big snows of the season, most of the snow had melted. But there were still patches of white to be found and snow angels to be made. There was fun to be had! Dolce and Amore love their walks with snow on the ground.

On the lookout for fresh snow, Malcolm and I took the girls on a new trail at the Galisteo Basin Preserve over the weekend. We knew the snow was getting thin, but certainly didn't anticipate the amount of mud we would encounter.

Snowmelt brings slush, and slush brings the mud. And more mud. And then more mud. Lots of mud. Thick gooey mud. Clay mud. As we swished and sloshed down the trail, more sliding than walking, we accumulated thick mud on our boots. The heavy mud dragged down our pace. Lesson learned, mud does not deter dogs.

Dolce and Amore took off like the wind. They smelled fun! They got a whiff of excitement and ran ahead like a bunch of banshees, barking for the sheer joy of dawggy play time! They didn't care about mud, only fun! What's a little mud between the paw pads when the air is chilly and there is snow to be found.

Dolce immediately sniffed out a sizable plot of snow under the Northern shade of a cluster of junipers. She immediately began her Shake, Rattle and Roll dance. It was Snow Angel time! Amore followed suit, building her own snow angel.

Dolce loves to make snow angels. She instinctively knows how to select the perfect patch of snow for rolling. She gauges the size, eyes the pristine surface area for protruding cacti and checks to identify if any other critters have already been in the area. She likes her snow to be untouched. Virgin snow. And she likes the snow to be on a slight incline.

Once Dolce gives the approval, the paws up okay signal, the girls jump in. Dolce and Amore start at the top end of the snowy incline, plop down and roll. Sliding head first, on their backs, they bite at the snow as they wiggle their hinnies into a slide down the incline. It's toboggan playtime! The steeper the incline, the better the ride n' slide. Malcolm and I call it their Shake, Rattle and Roll dance.

It's like a free ride at the fair. When they reach the bottom of the hill, where the snow meets mud, they hurry back up to the top of the patch to make another angel.

Then it's a race to the next patch of powder. They run through Juniper and Pinon, leaping over small gulleys and rain carved-out arroyos in search of more snow. They found it – along with a lot of mud, returning with mud-capped paws and more on their torso, chest and hind end.

Ooey gooey mud. Clay mud. Muck and uck!

The mud and the muck is worth it. The look on their faces, the expression in their eyes – there is nothing more joyful than watching them play and seeing unadulterated happiness shine back at you.

RULES

Coffee on Sunday mornings is a ritual. That, and the Sunday paper. It's our lazy day of sleeping in, catching up on a few household chores, and in general, not doing much.

That being said, we do have a few rules we follow: Starting with the first rule of the day: first one up starts the coffee.

Rule two: Same "first" one up, takes the dogs up the driveway to retrieve the 5 lbs. worth of circulars and ads called the Santa Fe New Mexican – the Sunday paper. No excuses. Bring some doggy biscuits to keep the girls from running off. Make them sit when receiving the treat. Bring both girls back to the house with the paper. Simple.

This means grabbing some dog treats to keep our two hellions in line as Dolce and Amore attempt to do more than just 'get-the-paper'. They sense freedom – early morning, first time out of the house freedom. Peanut Butter treats will keep the two from traveling afar, as their interest lay only with what's curled up within the treat-holding hand. PB Treats keep the girls from chasing bunnies and birds. Bring the treats.

Since I'm the one usually turning on the coffee and getting the paper, for the next hour or two, I purposely ignore the rest of the family rules....

Until Malcolm stumbles out of bed.

Obeying the Malcolm rule of "coffee before talkie," I mumble a low murmured, "Morn'in" and retreat back to what I was doing.

His replied greeting is equally low in tone, undistinguishable and usually interrupted by Dolce and Amore wanting their morning love. Dolce wiggling in between his legs for a back scratch, Amore jumping up for a hug.

Once the girls are satisfied with their Sunday morning lovin', Malcolm is allowed to grab a mug of coffee, settle down on the couch with the paper, sports section first, and start his day.

Malcolm calls this the organization rule. Leave him alone so he can get organized.

Organizational Rule: First the coffee – heavy cream, two heaping spoonfuls of dark brown sugar, a little cinnamon sprinkled on the top and nuked for 30 secs in the microwave. It is during the nuke session that he gives Dolce and Amore attention. They have thirty seconds of loving, but know when the microwave beeps; it's time to move back.

Following the organization phase, it's the subsequent couch prep rule. Pillows are arranged just so, the end table brought close enough for reach but far enough to avoid tail destruction of the coffee cup, and with an afghan thrown haphazardly over his lap, Malc is ready to scan the bold headlines found above the fold.

Malcolm is now organized. He is now prepped. Next up – the settling in rule. Let him get settled – then he'll function.

Settling in Rule: Once Malcolm is settled, the dogs are allowed to snuggle with him. Dolce and Amore move in for more love and loving. Amore knows at this point, one of them will be allowed up on the couch besides Malcolm's prone figure. The other gets to sit on the floor up against the sofa. They wait.

First come, first served is the girl's rule and it's usually Amore. She waits through all the organization, all the prep, all the settling in, through the pillow fluffing and the paper shuffling, through the blanket arrangement and small end table placement, waiting for her cue to join Malcolm on the couch. She knows the rules, after Malcolm's first sip of coffee she is cleared for lift off.

Amore springs up from her sitting position at the base of the couch, over Malcolm's prone form, and lands between the back of the couch and Malcolm's hip. Twists, turns and paws poking his belly, Amore snuggles in, draped over Malc's torso, head hanging by his side, her eyes closed in bliss. She beat Dolce to the punch. She has possession of both Malcolm and his lap.

If Malcolm is lucky, Amore has waited long enough on the couch jump for him to set his mug down, placed out of the way on the end table, to avoid hot coffee being spilled down his front.

If he is luckier, Amore's paws have landed on the couch cushion, missing his pride and joy, thus enabling Malcolm to walk and talk the rest of the day.

And if he is even luckier still, Amore will stay put for another 50-60 minutes, allowing Malcolm to avoid all rules and commands issued by said wife.

And now for the truth of all those other rules.....

With Amore's 100 pound frame pinning Malcolm down, Malcolm is able to circumvent any and all requests.

"Honey, would you....?" I start to ask.

"Can't, I have a dog on me!" Malcolm replies before I've even finished asking my request.

"It's your turn to...." I can't even finish my sentence before he interrupts me.

"Can't, I have a dog on me!" Malcolm quickly retorts back. He thinks because Amore is draped all over him he is pardoned from anything I might ask of him.

"Malc – you need to….." my voice sterner, I'm tired of the "I have a dog on me" excuse.

"Can't, I have a dog on me!" He laughs. Actually, it's a snicker. It was the snicker that did it. He's in trouble now. I didn't nag anymore. I don't yell or shout. I never say another word.

He thinks he is sooooo smart! Well, I was the youngest of four, tricked and picked on by three older siblings and I learned by the best! As the youngest, I had to out-smart my sisters. I had to out-do em'.

Listen up Malcolm – new rule – never try to out-trick a trickster.

The wife rule: By the third "can't, I have a dog on me," I calmly walked over to the treat jar, being sure to rattle the ceramic lid a good bit. That is all it takes, just one rattle of the treat jar. I waited. It didn't take long. A few seconds later and the dogs were on alert. Full alert. Their eyes latched on to me, following my movements. Waiting for the signal.

The ears on both dogs perked up to full attention, their bodies tense and ready for action. Their snouts wrinkling, sniffing the air, decoding the scents. They smell peanut butter.

Dogs will do anything for a tasty kibble. Especially a peanut butter treat. Once I had their attention, I gave the signal. A quick whistle had Amore and Dolce barreling through the living room, eager for their doggy treat. Dolce arriving first. Amore mere seconds later by default of having to unravel herself from Malcolm and the couch.

Another rule – never get between a dog and their treat.

The Treat Rule: Amore had to untangle herself from her snuggle-fest with Malcolm. Her front paws landing on his favored jewels, back legs gaining purchase on his belly, subsequently ripping the Op Ed section and his stomach to shreds before tipping over the end table. The race was on, who would get the peanut butter treat first.

It was the end table tip over that tossed the full of coffee mug off its perch, spewing nuked hot coffee all over Malcolm, then landing and breaking against the brick floor.

Oh, well! I shrugged off the loss. Personally, I never liked that mug anyway!

"ARRRUUUGHHH!" Those that know Malcolm, know his language was a lot more colorful and descriptive. That'll teach him!

I drop the nuggets into Amore and Dolce's waiting mouths. Their eyes shining from the unexpected treat, hoping for more. As I look over the back of the couch to Malcolm.

"What was that dear?" I asked him in a prepared sotto voice. I was not snarky at all. Okay, maybe just a little bit. Hee hee hee.

"Oh, and honey, now that you're up….."

Last rule to remember – and take note gentlemen, the wife always rules!

SANTA FE BITE
(a.k.a. BOBCAT BITE)

Traditionally, when family and friends come to visit, we treat our out-of-town guests to Bobcat Bite, or Bobcat's as I like to call it.

Bobcat's was an old trading post turned gun shop turned burger joint located halfway between our home and Santa Fe on Old Las Vegas Highway, the historic Route 66. A family owned business since 1953, Bobcat's was so named for the wild bobcats that came down from the surrounding mountains and were fed meat scraps and leftovers at the back door.

Bobcat's was owned by Bonnie and John, had only 5 small tables and a low long counter for singles and one-sie's. You paid with cash or check, no credit cards. If you didn't have enough on you to pay for dinner, Bonnie would vouch for you until your next visit to Bobcat's. You were given a Tootsie roll pop for dessert, kind of a dine and dash type of dessert, and those waiting for an empty table got restless if you lingered too long once you were finished with your meal.

A small chalkboard nailed by the front door held the names of the those next up for a table. The names at the top of the chalkboard got the first available table, those names on the bottom of the list, impatiently toe-tapped their annoyance in having to wait.

The menu changed little over the years, except perhaps they quit serving homemade fruit pie (guests took too long lingering over coffee and dessert). Burgers, steaks, and pork chops. Salad, garlic bread and country fries. Cole slaw, potato salad and skillet baked beans. Yummmmm!

A simple menu, but I can guaran-damn-tee you, it is the best burger you will ever have. Bar none. Ever. Ten ounces of ground daily choice sirloin and chuck, cooked to order on an old handmade cast iron griddle, it is a two-fisted burger, bookended by a specially baked sourdough bun and served with potato chips. That's it.

The first bite was a jaw-breaker, only because it was so huge, so tall in height, it was hard to wrap your mouth around. The last bite was an assembly of hamburger pieces, broken potato chips and bits of green chili that fell out of the burger onto the paper-lined burger basket. You never wanted to waste a bite.

I liked the green chili cheeseburger, rare-to-medium rare, raw onions, no chips. Malcolm would order the green chili cheese, medium, onions, two tomato slices, lettuce, yes on the chips and the potato salad on the side, but only if Bonnie made the potato salad. The others in the kitchen didn't cook the potatoes long enough.

We learned to flip the burger upside down as soon as it arrived so the juices gravitated into new territory, spreading the succulent flavors throughout. What we couldn't eat we saved for the girls. Tiamo, Dolce and Amore enjoyed the leftovers minus the onions and green chili.

Best damn burger! Ever!

When it was just Tiamo, we would bring her with us, sitting outside at a small bistro-styled table on their portal. Tiamo would lay under the table at our feet, occasionally being handed scraps of hamburger when Malcolm wasn't watching. Bonnie would wrap up our leftovers for Tiamo to snack on later. Tiamo was in hamburger heaven.

Tiamo learned at a young age if we turned left at the blinking light where Hwys 285 and Old Las Vegas met up, it was a Bobcat night and a sure bet she would get a Bobcat treat. She would go from zero to wildly excited before we even rounded the corner. Tiamo loved Bobcat's. Loved sitting outside under the table with us on the portal. Loved being fed little bites of hamburger when Malcolm wasn't looking.

Should we turn a quarter of a mile early, getting on the freeway, Tiamo sulked in the back corner of the car all the way into town. Tiamo would mope and pout once she realized Bobcat's was not on the agenda.

When Dolce and Amore came along, we would leave the three dogs in the car in Bobcat's parking lot while we enjoyed our meal. Every so often, we would hear loud barks from the girls, encouraging us to hurry it up. They knew Bonnie had wrapped up our leftovers and there were meat scraps to be had.

Typically, repeat houseguests will request a Bobcat burger upon their return to Santa Fe, telling us they've been craving Bobcat's since they started planning their trip. On occasion, they will demand to come back for a second round of burgers before they leave town – sort of a "one for the road" talisman.

Today, Bobcat Bite is now Santa Fe Bite. No longer housed in the old trading post on Old Las Vegas Highway, Santa Fe Bite has moved into town and is located just down the street from the Round House, our State Capital.

Bonnie and John still own the joint. The burgers are still the best damn hamburgers. Ever! I still order the green chili cheeseburger, rare-to-medium-rare, onions, no chips. Malcolm still asks who made the potato salad before ordering a side. Beer and wine have been added to the menu, along with a few other dishes. The potato chips are now house-made and Tootsie roll pops are still offered for dessert. Still the same, yet boasting a new address.

The girls certainly don't mind the move into town, they still get our leftovers. Or in their case, the doggy bag!

~~RECIPE~~ (strike that) RULES FOR A SANTA FE BITE BURGER

- Drive fast, dangerously fast, to Santa Fe Bite to arrive before the other patrons; believe you me, this is serious business.
- Run, don't walk, to the new front check-in podium and get your name down on the waiting list. Get your name down before those out-of-town tourists have a chance to get out of the car and figure out the new waiting system.
- While waiting for a table, give a hard stare to the lingering patrons, intimidating those slow poke customers into speeding up their meal. This isn't Paris, they don't get to dawdle over coffee.
- Once seated, read the menu quickly and know what you want – don't dilly-daddle. There are people waiting for your table – like us – plus, you don't want to delay that first bite of your burger. Eat up folks!
- Inquire who boiled the potatoes that morning (just kidding John). If Bonnie made the potato salad, be sure to order a side of it. It's the good kind of potato salad. Better than mom made.
- Order and enjoy the best damn burger ever, ever, ever! This is no ordinary burger – hold on to your socks kiddos, you're in for a treat!
- Ask for more napkins, you're gonna need 'em – now ask for another one. Just in case you need more. Keep a spare for emergencies. Tuck one in the collar of your shirt. Ask

for two more napkins. Place these two on you lap, one for each thigh. Hide one in your purse for later. You think I'm joking, don't you! Ha! Just wait til you go to Santa Fe Bite yourself.

- Discreetly undo the snap on your jeans, pulling your shirt out and over to cover the opening. Okay, now you have more room to indulge in your burger – oh, yeah, and you can breathe. Next time, wear pants with an elastic waistband. Or better yet, wear a bathrobe that you can let out with a slip of the tie. Don't worry, you'll learn.

- Eat, pay and grab your Tootsie pop as you exit, you can enjoy it in the car on the way home. Please leave now so your table can be reset - Malcolm and I are next on the waiting list.

- Save your left-overs for your own doggy. Your dog will love you for life! Be sure to scrape off the green chili and any onion.

- Start planning your next visit to Santa Fe Bite'

http://www.santafebite.com

BUFFY

The City of Paris Dry Goods Company's Christmas tree, is a Christmas tree so big, it reaches the top floor! Five stories high. For a small child, a tree so big, it was unbelievable. It was Christmas magic.

When I was little nipper, every November, my mother would take us kids into San Francisco to go shopping. Christmas Shopping. This was major get out the card, shop til' ya drop, type of shopping. In one day, in one fell swoop, get'er all done kind of shopping.

We lived in a small farming community in Central California, so a trip to San Francisco meant a grand adventure for my sisters and me. It meant having a fancy lunch and if we were lucky some See's Chocolate. It meant a ride on the cable car and some salt water taffy candy down at the wharf. It meant seeing the Golden Gate Bridge and huge ships in the bay. It meant a fun day away from chores. Yippee!

But a shopping trip in November meant going to the City of Paris Department Store and seeing their five-story tall Christmas tree, a true wonderland for my young eyes.

I remember one year, all of us kids got new Christmas togs. New, not a hand-me-down-four-times-doesn't-quite-fit-it's-too-short Christmas dress, but a brand new dress. New, not home-made or sewn, but with tags still attached new. A Christmas dress from the City of Paris. All of us kids were excited. A special dress for each of us. Life was never so good.

I still remember that dress. It was blue with red xylophone bars across the front and down to the hem line, gold cording over the bars. It was a Buffy dress.

TV's Family Affair's, Buffy Davis wore one just like it on the show. Oh, how I loved that show and oh, how I loved that dress. At the time, I was six and a half, pudgy with freckles across my nose, a scraggly pixie hair cut and missing two front teeth.

Not exactly the cutest kid in the class, but when I put on my Buffy dress, I magically transformed into a princess. A Buffy princess.

I've always believed, at some point, young or old, every little girl and every older woman needs a Buffy dress. Something that makes their inner self shine, something that lets them feel beautiful and special, inside and out.

The other day, while at the Eldorado Country Pet Store, I found the perfect Holiday outfits for Dolce and Amore. I couldn't resist. I had to have them.

They were dark red velveteen doggy collars with several little shinny gold bells sewn throughout. They slipped right over the head, staying in place with a little elastic sewn within the fabric of the collar.

The dark red was beautiful against Dolce and Amore 's black fur. It contrasted well with their white chest and their Swiss cross markings. The collars were to be their Christmas apparel.

I didn't care that Malcolm might get just a tiny bit cranky over some frivolous doggy purchase. Nope. Come hell or high water, I was buying. I had found the ideal Buffy attire for them. Something to make them feel beautiful. Special. Like a Buffy dog princess.

When I arrived home, I couldn't wait to have Dolce and Amore try on their Christmas outfits. I was excited to surprise Malcolm. I called the girls out to the garage to put on their collars.

I wasn't sure what either would do with the velveteen collar, a foreign object that jingled and wrapped around their necks. I had a brief horrified thought that they would hate the feel of the elastic around their necks and start pawing to "get-it-off." I fleetingly wondered if the shinny bells would bother them. If the sweet twinkling sound would irritate their ears. I didn't think twice that once dog hair adhered to the velveteen fabric that I wouldn't be able to return the beautiful collars. At this point they were going to love them because I wanted them to love em'.

Dolce and Amore had never donned dog clothes before. They wore leather dog collars with their tags. That's it. Those collars never came off of them. They had their harnesses for hikes and trips into town. The girls knew the propose of the harness. But never had they dressed in holiday apparel. This would be a new adventure for them.

The moment of truth arrived. I said a quick prayer as I slipped on their collars. I crossed my fingers, I held my breath.

Dolce was first. She gave a little shake of her head, listening to the jingle jangle of the tiny bells as the collar settled on her neckline. She didn't seem to mind the collar too much. In fact, she seemed to like the special attire. She shook the velveteen collar again and again to hear the tinkle of the little sleigh bells. She liked it.

So far, so good. Amore was next. Always the problem child, I had no idea if Amore would like the idea of a fancy collar or give me grief for trying.

I could tell Amore didn't quite know what to make of the collars. She glanced over at Dolce, who was taking it all in stride. Would she fight it, or would she accept her fate, wearing a red velveteen collar?

I held out the collar, opening up the elastic to slip it over her head. The next thing I saw was Amore's head pushing up through the opening and the red collar was surrounding her décolletage. She liked it! She didn't just like the collar, she loved it! Both girls loved their red velveteen collars with the little bells sewn throughout.

Dolce loved her Buffy collar so much she wouldn't let me take it off her. She pranced and danced, loving the sound of the tiny bells attached to the collar. She would bob her neck and head just to hear the little bells ring. Her inner Buffy princess was doing the happy dance.

Amore carried her collar through out the house. I think she liked the jingle jangle from the little bells as well. When it came time to remove the collars she tucked her head down, refusing to let me detach it.

And Malcolm, he grabbed the camera to take pictures of our beautiful princesses. He thought the collars perfect canine attire for the holidays!

Here's to the Buffy in all of us!

GOLDILOCKS

Growing up, my father had a big ol' over-stuffed brown leather chair. His chair and matching ottoman were positioned just so — enabling him to watch our black & white console television at just the right angle. That was *HIS* chair.

All the dirty rubber bands from the evening newspapers, his toothpicks, his torn-out magazine articles, his dog-eared paperbacks, collected on, in or by, *HIS* chair.

If one of us girls happened to be sitting in *HIS* chair when he came in the living room to watch the telly or to read the evening paper, we had to vamoose. Quickly! Out of *HIS* chair lickety-split, forfeiting all rights to the seat.

Saturday mornings, my sisters and I would dig through the chair sides, under the seat cushion, searching for loose change. Coins that had slipped out of his denim pockets throughout the week as he sunk further into the chair while watching T.V.

On a good week, we could net a hefty profit, easily tripling our paltry allowance. Most times, it was a bust. The fun was in digging for treasure in *HIS* chair.

The years brought longer afternoon naps and more cracks to the aging dried out leather. The worn seat sagged way below the equator. The arm rests wiggled and giggled better than Jell-O, but stayed put with extra nails pounded into the chair frame. Still, it was *HIS* chair. Worn down, broken-in, and mighty comfortable, that chair was dad's and always would be.

Tiamo had a "special chair" as well. Our Kilim rug covered ottoman-slash-coffee table on steroids. As a puppy, the overly large ottoman was the only piece of furniture low enough in height for her to climb up. Our Kilim ottoman ended up being *HER* chair.

All of ten weeks old, Tiamo would put her front snow-capped paws on the top edge of the large oversized ottoman, her short little hind legs furiously working from below to gain purchase, as she learned how to pull herself up to the top of the ottoman. Where victory lay. The gold medal within reach.

There she lay, eyes sparkling from her achievement as she reached the summit. With the added height of the ottoman, Tiamo was another foot taller. Tiamo had conquered the ottoman and laid claim to it. That ottoman became *HER* chair.

Since the day she reached the ottoman summit, that ottoman was hers and hers alone. If someone happened to be encroaching on her ottoman, a bark and a paw nudge was usually enough to get them to move along to another location. She didn't care where, just not on her ottoman. It was *HER* chair. It didn't matter if she wanted to sit there herself or not, it was *HER* chair. Off with those that didn't understand that.

Tiamo wasn't aggressive about it. She was more passive when removing someone from *HER* special chair, gentle even. Both Malcolm and I have experienced Tiamo literally pushing us off her spot, leaning with all her body weight until we gave in and let her have her ottoman back.

On weekends, I would scoot the ottoman next to the couch, where I read the Sunday paper. Tiamo would lay down on *HER* chair, her head inches away from me as I curled up on the sofa with a lap blanket sipping my morning coffee, reading the news. She loved being next to me while still on *HER* chair.

When the puppies were born, Tiamo's ottoman became more and more sacred. Tiamo became more territorial with her special place. Momma had staked her claim to the ottoman years prior and no little whippersnapper, no little puppy, even if they were her children, was going to poach on it.

Amore and Dolce eventually learned to leave the ottoman to Tiamo. The only trespasser allowed on the ottoman, was Thugs, our cat at the time, with whom Tiamo had grown up and had always been protective. On cold days, Thugs would often curl up against Tiamo on the ottoman, enjoying the warmth from Tiamo's body. Thugs was the only one allowed access to *HER* chair.

When Tiamo passed, Malcolm and I wondered who would be the first to take over the ottoman, claiming the ottoman as theirs. Dolce or Amore? Both had tried repeatedly throughout the years when Tiamo was alive, but to no avail. It was *HER* chair.

My bet was on Dolce, as Amore has always preferred the cold brick floor under her belly. Malcolm thought it might be Amore as she only likes something she can't have.

So far, neither has shown any desire to acquire the ottoman as "theirs." It sits empty to this day. I believe the girls see the ottoman as *HER* chair. Tiamo's.

Amore has jumped over it, using the ottoman as a hurdle. Dolce has used the ottoman as a launching pad to chase after Amore, but the girls have yet to enjoy their afternoon nap on Tiamo's ottoman, stretched out with the sun warming their belly. Dolce and Amore both recognize the Kilim ottoman as Tiamo's. It was *HER* chair. Even Gordita has kept her distance from Tiamo's ottoman.

Malcolm and I both believe, in their minds, it will always be Tiamo's special chair.

LIKE MOTHER, LIKE DAUGHTER

Growing up, I would cringe when I heard the words, "you take after your father." Or better yet, "you look just like your mom." Ew! Who wants to looks like their mother?

At fifteen, I did not want to be compared to either parent. I only saw dad as hosting a big nose and a larger belly. And my mother? Well, suffice to say, I did not want to grow up to be like my mother. I wanted to be me. Just me.

Only now do I understand those words were sweet compliments full of promise of what was to come. My parents' moral fiber had been imprinted on me in my early years. Their love and emotional support has stayed with me even with their passing, years ago. Today, I would consider it a wonderful testament to my parents should I hear those same words again.

Now, at full maturity and with a clear mirror, I see a bit of both my parents in me, from partaking of my father's gift of gab and love of a busy social life to sharing my mother's propensity to uphold her Scandinavian heritage – being a stubborn Swede on occasion. Okay, according to Malcolm, more than on occasion.

I've copied my father's coloring, having fair-hair and blue eyes, and I took on my mom's easy-going manner. I share my father's love of cooking and my mother's enjoyment of travel. I followed in my both my parents' footsteps and started my own catering business. Today, how could I not be "just like my parents?"

I find myself mimicking their mannerisms, their habits and their likes and dislikes. Things like buying only French's mustard and Best Food's mayo and using only real butter, because that's what my mother kept in the cupboards. Like mother, like daughter.

I find myself modeling my business practices after my father. Replicating his habits and applying the same standards and ethics as dad would have. I've decided I'm just like my dad. It's not such a bad thing.

With dogs, all traits and characteristics are individual. They might share looks, the same blaze on the forehead, the same white-capped paws, but all similarities end there. Their personalities are all their own. It's not environmental, it's not genetic, it's not because of their sire or parent. Puppies don't take after their mama, nor do they act just like their sire. Canine personalities are distinct and singular.

I once had a dog trainer inform me, "Dogs do not learn from other dogs, they learn from repetitive learning and rewards."

I used to believe that, now I'm not so sure……

When Tiamo was just a puppy, she would prance a little jig as we walked her. She had a special spring in her gait, unique to just her. I'd never seen another dog with the same perky step, the same dance. Like a model on the catwalk, Tiamo had a sway all her own.

Until, just the other day – as Malcolm and I were walking the girls, I noticed Dolce dancing a little jig, so like Tiamo. She had the same perky step, the same sway as Tiamo. That same dance. Had Dolce learned her little dancing strut, the special spring in her gait, from Tiamo? Or was it just one of her mannerisms?

Tiamo had a habit of holding her head up, tucking her muzzle in, and looking up at you with a shy, Princess Di gaze. She was so graceful, so like royalty. She was so serene. Regal.

Recently, I saw Amore lift her head and tuck in her muzzle, as she peered up at me, similar to Shy Di. In that instant, that flash of a moment, she looked so much like Tiamo, she took my breath away. Did Amore pick up her regal look from Tiamo?

Tiamo had a special spot under the table, where she would lay as we ate dinner, her front paws draped over my toes, just to let me know she was there. Now Amore lays there, in the exact spot as Tiamo, her right paw touching my left foot, so like Tiamo. The same paw, the same foot. The same touch.

On trail, Dolce walks behind us in our wake, just like Tiamo. She stops to sniff out the neighborhood, see what's going on, sniff to determine what's new, just like Tiamo did. She double backs to grab a horse apple, gobbling it down quickly, just like Tiamo did. She'll drop her head in embarrassed shame when in trouble, just like Tiamo did.

Malcolm and I have found many of Tiamo's characteristics and behaviors imprinted onto Amore and Dolce. We see countless mannerisms in the girls that parallel Tiamo's. We notice numerous gestures and affectations of Tiamo's that Dolce and Amore mimic. We see the signs of Tiamo in both of them. Like mother, like daughter.

We certainly didn't teach Dolce how to prance a little jig when walking the loop. We definitely didn't encourage Dolch to eat horse apples. There was no way we could have taught Amore to tuck in her muzzle and peer up at me like Tiamo use to. We didn't make Amore sit under the table with her paw on my foot.

Is it learned behavior? Is it genetics? Is it environment? Or is it just being a dog, instinctive mannerisms?

Malcolm and I find ourselves saying, "Dolce acts just like Tiamo" or "She is so like her mother," something every teenager hates to hear. Amore has always "looked" more like Tiamo – Dolce has always behaved more like Tiamo. Both have taken on traits only Tiamo possessed.

Like mother, like daughters.

QUESTERS OF THE TRUTH

I was eight when I found myself at the crossroads of Christmas belief. The perilous intersection where believing in Santa meets the acceptance of reality.

I hung on with child-like confidence that my schoolyard friends were mistaken, my older siblings were wrong, that there truly was a Santa and reindeer and the North Pole. Elves and a real toy factory. I didn't like being laughed at for 'still' believing. Santa had to be real. I desperately wanted him to be real, but I definitely didn't want to be the last one to learn the truth.

My parents subscribed to the holiday charade of Santa, giving credence to my conviction in Mr. Claus. Candy filled stockings, milk and cookies for Santa, even hay for the reindeer were utter proof to my young years that Santa Claus was real. Whispered, "better be good for Santa" rang in my ears, while Holiday carols spewed from the car radio. Everywhere I turned was evidence that Santa existed. How dare my classmates tease me that there wasn't a Santa Claus!

Every member of our family had a red felt stocking, handmade by our mother, with our names sewn on the top. They hung on the wooden mantle above the fireplace just waiting to be filled by the jolly ol' man himself. Even our family dogs had specially stitched stockings that were bursting with rawhide treats by Christmas morn. I certainly didn't want Santa to go away, leaving me an empty stocking. If I didn't believe, would Santa skip our house? Would our stockings be packed away, never again to be filled chockfull of candy and toys?

On the eve of Christmas, my mother would assist my sisters and I in placing a tall glass of milk and a plate of homemade cookies on the hearth, our carefully handwritten wish lists arranged by its side. Snicker doodles, Russian wedding cakes, candy cane cookies piled high on a large red platter, tasty treats for St. Nick.

For weeks prior, Mother could be found in the kitchen, baking the most wonderful holiday confections; letting each of us kids select our favorite cookie to make. If I didn't believe in Santa, would mother quit baking sweets, my eight-year old brain frantically wondered? Would the warm cinnamon scent waffling through the house fade away? Would there be no special dessert served after our Christmas Day dinner? Would we still celebrate Christmas?

A few days before Christmas, Father would bring home a huge bale of hay.

"Fodder for the reindeer," he'd grunt, as he was hefting the heavy bale from the back of the pickup truck.

Under the bright outdoor Christmas lights, he'd scatter the flakes of hay about the front yard. Eight large hay mounds tagged for the reindeer pulling Santa's sleigh and a special one for Rudolf. Once he directed us to place apples on top of the alfalfa claiming they needed extra energy for their long night delivering presents around the world. If I didn't believe in Santa Claus, who would feed the reindeer? Would Christmas go away? Would anyone care?

For forty some-odd years, I've sat at the junction of believing and not-quite believing. Do I continue on the magical journey, keeping my faith in the magic of Santa? Do I take a sharp right turn, jostling the memories of filled stockings, homemade cookies and hay for the reindeer before packing them tightly away in the trunk? One year the decision was taken out of my hands.

A few years back, Malcolm and I were asked to play Mr. and Mrs. Claus for friends of ours hosting a large family Christmas gathering. We were given a beautiful Santa suit, specially selected presents for the children, and directions on where and when to show up. My husband practiced his "Ho Ho Ho" while I made a list of all the "good" children's names that would be attending.

The bright red Santa suit was fur trimmed and was embellished with tall black boots, a wide thick belt, and a red velvet hat. White woolen gloves, a snow-white beard and hairpiece, old-fashioned wire-rimmed glasses along with a padded under belly pillow completed the costume.

As Malcolm was dressing for the part, our two Bernese Mountain Dogs came in to investigate, sniffing at the strange red velvet material and pristine fur adorning the edges. I grabbed the camera, begging Malcolm to sit with the dogs for a brief photo op and quickly snapped some pictures before we needed to be on our way.

It was weeks later that I remembered to upload the pictures to the computer. January was getting ready to turn into February before I had the time to flip through the pictures I had taken. Christmas had long passed, the tree taken down, the holiday decorations put away. The spirit of Christmas had disappeared into worrying about paying the bills. I sat at the computer and pulled up the pictures from Christmas.

Jeffrey Moussaieff Masson once said, "Questers of the truth, that's who dogs are; seekers after the invisible scent of another being's authentic core." I looked at the first photo on the screen, seeing our two Berners with Santa.

The opening photo revealed our dogs, Dolce and Amore, nestled beside Santa, one on each side, gazing up at him with wonder. They were enchanted with Father Christmas, enthralled with his inner spirit, his big heart, his jolly laugh. The adoration in their eyes shone with true belief. Santa's authentic core was laid bare by the truest of seekers. And, there was my Santa, eyes closed, basking in the joy of unselfish affection and unconditional love.

I knew without a doubt, weeks into the new year when Christmas was a long past a remembrance, it didn't matter whether you are a just turned eight year old or way past the half-century mark, Santa was real and would be forever.

MEMORIES

No story. No cute anecdote of the girls. No humorous tale of Dolce sitting on my lap or Amore stealing the Kong. No ramblings relating to the storyline. No deep meaning words of wisdom, quip, or quote.

This is just about memories of our Tiamo. Remembering the softness in her eyes, her tender nudge with her muzzle to get our attention, her gentleness when she would tend to her litter. Tiamo tenderly pawing us, leaning against us, licking us.

It's about reminiscing how she would con me into giving her nightly belly rubs, every night, for six years straight. It's about her joy to be with us on road trips and trips to the grocery store. It's about her companionship to Malcolm and myself and her unconditional love for her "pack."

It's about her protectiveness with Thugs, following her at a close distance to keep her safe when outside. It's about how she would flirt with the big male Berners, and show disdain to the little lap dogs, though she was a lap lover herself.

Malcolm and I often play the "remember when" game. Remember when Tiamo would counter-surf and steal the cookies.

I would blame Malcolm for sneaking a cookie off the cooling rack, when all the time it was Tiamo.

Remember when Tiamo would start barking at 5:10 p.m. on the dot, wanting out the front door to wait for me to drive in from work. She knew I was due home soon and wanted to wait for me in the front portal, running immediately to the car door as soon as I turned the engine off.

Remember when Tiamo would bust out of the dog pen and run around to the back porch, pawing at the door to get back inside – how she hated being separated from us. We abandoned that pen for two years until the puppies were born and finally Tiamo accepted that pen.

Other times we play the "remember how" game. Remember how Tiamo would lay her head on my lap, her paw on my leg when she was tired, and other times she would lean so close to us, we were supporting her full weight.

Remember how Tiamo would give us big bear hugs, her huge paws wrapping around our waist, squeezing us hard. We knew better than to have her jump on us, and yet, we still let her, even encouraging her. We just loved her hugs!

Remember how we swore we would never, ever let her on our bed. And, for two years we didn't, until I broke down after Sam had died and literally picked her up, placed her on my side of the mattress and cuddled with her. Needing her solace just as she needed ours. From then on, Tiamo slept with us, giving us her love.

Our "remember whens" and our "remember hows" usually end with a saddened, "oh, how I miss her." Malcolm and I will share a tender smile full of Tiamo memories. Once in a while, a teardrop will slip past my armor, Malcolm nodding in understanding, silently acknowledging our bittersweet memories. I miss her hugs. Our cuddles. Our belly rubs.

Oh, how I miss her.

.

ABOUT THE AUTHOR

Born on the Central Coast of California, Megan McFarlane made her move to the southwest many years ago where she resides in Santa Fe, New Mexico with her husband and their very large, 100-pounds each, Bernese Mountain Dogs, along with one, very fat cat, named Gordita.

Megan McFarlane is the author of *If It Falls on the Floor, It's Mine!* A cookbook filled with canine love and laughter. Available at Amazon.

For more tails of the dogs, go to: www.ifitfallsonthefloor.com

www.ingramcontent.com/pod-product-compliance
Lightning Source LLC
La Vergne TN
LVHW020055090426
835513LV00029B/1476